THE
GARDENS OF
PORTUGAL

THE GARDENS OF PORTUGAL

HELENA ATTLEE

PHOTOGRAPHS BY
JOHN FERRO SIMS

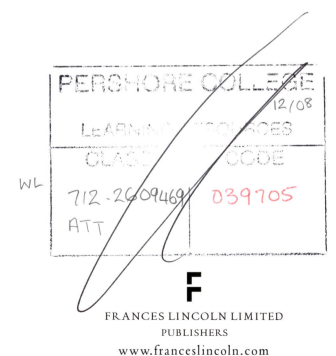
F

FRANCES LINCOLN LIMITED
PUBLISHERS
www.franceslincoln.com

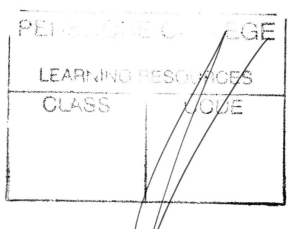

FOR MY SISTER, LIZ GREENE

Frances Lincoln Ltd
4 Torriano Mews
Torriano Avenue
London NW5 2RZ
www.franceslincoln.com

Commissioned and edited by Jane Crawley
Designed by Ian Hunt

HALF-TITLE Late-nineteenth-century mosaic decorating the bath house in the garden of Quinta da Regaleira.
TITLE The colourful façade of Casa da Pergola in Cascais.

CONTENTS

PREFACE

LEFT *The lush forest of Mata do Bussaco. This is the area surrounding the Fonte Fria, a dramatic water staircase designed in the mid-nineteenth century by Marcellino and Giuseppe Roda, Italian landscape architects, for Queen Maria Pia.*

ABOVE *A white camellia begins to flower in October in the garden of Casa da Ínsua.*

JOHN FERRO SIMS would like to thank the Portuguese National Tourist Office – U.K and its regional offices for their invaluable help on this wonderful project. He would also like to thank the private garden owners who have often had to struggle to maintain their unique national heritage.

Thousands of visitors are drawn to Portugal each year but few of them visit its gardens. Their loss is your gain. The gardens are rarely crowded and the arrival of foreign visitors is often a special event for garden owners, who can be particularly welcoming and enthusiastic. Some gardens will draw you away from the main road, leading you into areas of the country that are rarely seen by visitors. Occasionally the gardens are difficult to locate but, armed with a good map, you will find that the search enriches your experience of Portugal.

There is much to interest the plantsman in Portugal. Tender plants thrive in the mild climate, and warmth combined with high annual rainfall and generous supplies of natural spring water produces gardens that are surprisingly lush throughout the year. Many gardens were generated when the baroque was at its most flamboyant, but there is also a superb modern landscape to be seen in Porto at the Parque de Serralves.

The visiting season is unusually long. It begins in January when flowering camellias light up gardens in the north of the country. The camellia season continues until March. In June and September moderate heat combines with a wonderful quality of light. Whatever month you choose, it is important to remember that northern and central Portugal have an Atlantic climate. You should be prepared for rain at all times of year. Summer temperatures can soar, but the weather changes surprisingly fast.

The gardens in this book are arranged alphabetically in two sections. The first covers Coimbra and the gardens to the north of it, while all the gardens in the second section lie to the south of Coimbra. Some of the gardens are public and others belong to hotels and guest houses. There are also several private gardens that can only be seen by appointment. English is fairly widely spoken, but if you have difficulties making an appointment you might enlist the help of the local tourist board. There are details on pages 18–19 for every garden mentioned here and on page 171 you will find a list of the books that I have found useful.

I would like to extend sincere thanks to all of the owners who have allowed their gardens to be included in this book. Many people have been generous with their time and expertise, but I would particularly like to thank Gerald Luckhurst for his unfailing kindness in sharing his own research and expert knowledge; the Portuguese branch of the Mediterranean Garden Society, and especially Marion ter Horst for her invaluable help and enthusiasm; Ben Weijers, Emelia Ribeiro, and the Anglo-Portuguese Institute in London.

INTRODUCTION

Imagine a garden in a dream, a place at once familiar and deeply strange. This is the curious sensation evoked by Portuguese gardens. Architectural forms borrowed from France, Italy and England bring familiarity, but they sit alongside exotic features introduced by the Arabs who settled Portugal in the eighth century. So are these derivative gardens? Gardens that owe a little to everyone and own nothing themselves? Not at all. Portugal is a crucible. Beneath burning summer suns and in the teeth of damp Atlantic gales these diverse elements have fused to form something unique and distinctly Portuguese.

Portuguese gardens were built predominantly in the sixteenth and eighteenth centuries. They were the expression of a wonderful sense of well-being generated by the country's most glorious moments of economic and colonial achievement. The first of these two golden ages occurred at the beginning of the sixteenth century. By the end of the fifteenth century Portuguese navigators had already pioneered sea routes to India and the Orient, and Portugal – a small, medieval nation on the edge of Europe – began to trade globally. A steady stream of Portuguese cargo ships made the gruelling voyage around the Cape of Good Hope, returning home with priceless cargoes of pepper, cinnamon, cloves, nutmeg, cardamom pods, turmeric and mace, African gold and oriental silks. Portugal was rapidly transformed into one of the richest countries in Europe. The court of Dom Manuel I – 'the Fortunate' (1495–1521) – exerted a magnetic force, drawing artists, sculptors and architects to Portugal from all over Europe. The houses of this period were richly and exotically decorated with intensely-coloured tiles and gilded wood, oriental silks, Chinese porcelain and woven-silk wall hangings from India. Fashionable new gardens adorned the exterior of these houses, but very few of them are extant today. The only important garden to survive from the sixteenth century is at Quinta da Bacalhoa in Azeitão (see page 114) where Italianate loggias and parterre beds cohabit with a magnificent Moorish water tank and an abundance of the *azulejos*, or glazed tiles, that became one of the salient features of the Portuguese garden.

The country's first golden age lasted barely fifty years. The first flush of riches passed, and then the Portuguese army was disastrously defeated by the Moroccans at the Battle of Alcacer Kibir (1578). Many of the aristocracy were obliged to sell jewels, gold and even silver tableware to pay the cost of the war and the ransom on fathers, brothers, uncles and cousins held prisoner in Morocco. Between 1581 and

During the seventeenth century Portuguese tiles, or azulejos*, began to be combined to create rectangular panels or tableaux in the garden. The irregular shape of this* azulejos *decoration in the garden of Casa da Santar is unusual.*

1640 Portugal was under Spanish rule. The wars of the restoration of Portuguese independence (1641–68) dominated the middle years of the century and gardens, symptoms of a better time, ceased to be built.

The second golden age was fuelled by the discovery first of gold and then diamonds in Brazil. Once again the King of Portugal – this time Dom João V (1706–50) – was one of the richest sovereigns in Europe. Portugal was gripped by the frenzy of the first modern gold rush. Thousands of young men, and sometimes entire families, emigrated to Brazil. They often returned with fortunes that they invested in land, establishing wine-growing estates and building fine *quintas*, or manor houses, and fashionable gardens. Many of the greatest houses in northern Portugal – like Casa da Ínsua (see page 66) – date from this period. Several new palaces and gardens also sprang up in and around Lisbon – Palácio de Fronteira being one of the finest examples (see page 130).

The Portuguese give a variety of titles to their houses. *Casa*, simply meaning 'house', can be applied to a really large and ornate building like Casa da Ínsua. *Palácio* is generally reserved for true palaces, and the word can sometimes be abbreviated to *paço*. A *solar* is a fine house used both as a pleasure palace and a farmhouse, rather in the tradition of the ancient Roman *villa*. *Quinta*, the most common title for a rural house with a garden, is used to refer both to a manor house and to the estate that surrounds it.

BELOW LEFT *Dappled sunlight falls on the courtyard of Casa da Ínsua. The main entrance to the house is to the right. Inside, the hall is decorated with spears, arrows and fishermen's cane baskets, curiosities brought back from Brazil at the end of the eighteenth century by Luís de Albuquerque de Mello Pereira. The family chapel predates the house. Its seventeenth-century façade is visible beyond the fountain.*

BELOW RIGHT *Granite is the indigenous stone of northern Portugal. It was generally used in gardens for statues, like this at Casa da Ínsua, planting troughs, benches, gate piers and fountains. It is a dense and unforgiving medium that makes hard work for sculptors. Consequently the stonework in northern Portugal tends to be relatively simple.*

This elegant seventeenth-century manor house stands high above the Lima valley. It has belonged to the Calheiros family ever since it was built and it is one of the finest buildings in the area. There is no real logic to the naming of Portuguese buildings, and this one is called the Paço de Calheiros, or Calheiros Palace. Today, the Count of Calheiros runs the house as a small hotel.

The devastating earthquake of 1755 destroyed many gardens in Lisbon and the surrounding area, and more were lost in the second half of the century during the Marquis de Pombal's persecution of the aristocracy. James Murphy toured Portugal during this period. His official purpose was a survey of interesting buildings, but he did not fail to observe the aristocracy, giving a vivid account of their lives against the background of these dramatic events. 'The nobility … are not very rich', he says:

> … for tho' their patrimonies are large, their rents are small. I doubt if any of them has ever seen a map of his estate or exactly knows its boundaries … In a country wherein there are no racehorses, no licensed gambling houses or expensive mistresses, a gentleman may live splendidly on a moderate income … Nor do they excite the envy of the poor by midnight orgies or gilded chariots. Their time is spent between their duty at court and the social enjoyments of private parties. … Their lives are an even tenor of domestic felicities, not remarkable for brilliant actions, and but rarely stained by vice … They possess many amiable qualities. They are religious, temperate and generous, faithful to their friends, charitable to the distressed and warmly attached to their sovereign, whose approbation and a peaceful retirement constitute the greatest happiness of their lives.

The nineteenth century saw a series of upheavals in Portugal. The country was invaded three times by the French between 1807, when the entire royal court fled to Brazil, and 1811. Naturally, there were no gardens made during French occupation,

or in its immediate aftermath. There was a slight revival of interest at the end of the civil war in 1834, when the new liberal aristocracy returned from their exile abroad, bringing with them novel ideas about the landscape style of gardening. By this time the country was scattered with empty convents and monasteries, and these magnificent buildings were sometimes bought by private owners who renovated or rebuilt the gardens in their grounds. The romantic, naturalistic garden was made fashionable by Ferdinand Saxe-Coburg-Gotha, Queen Maria II's German husband, who built a 494-acre (200-hectare) park on the hill between the Pena Palace and Sintra. The park, built between 1846 and 1885, incorporated the naturally dramatic features of the precipitous site into a highly romantic layout of gardens within gardens that were adorned with picturesque buildings and connected by a network of narrow paths and carriage drives. The bare hillside was planted with a thicket of trees and shrubs, many of them imported from Japan, New Zealand, Brazil and North America. Camellias grew in the valley at the base of the hill, and close by a grove of tree ferns still thrives in the damp shade. The king set up the Royal Company of Asphalt, and consequently this unlikely substance was used as a rare and precious material throughout the garden. The gardener in charge of this extraordinary landscape was Jean Baptiste Bonnard, a Frenchman who had also worked in Italy.

Portugal continued to find inspiration abroad for its garden landscapes throughout the nineteenth and the twentieth centuries. In 1895 António Augusto Carvahlo Monteiro began the transformation of Quinta da Regaleira in Sintra by first taking advice from the Parisian architect Henri Lusseau, and then commissioning Luigi Manini, an Italian set designer, to make plans for a new palace and garden surrounding it (see page 160). In 1932 Carlos Alberto Cabral, Count of Vizela, followed a similar route, commissioning the French architect Jacques Gréber to design the landscape around Casa de Serralves in Porto (see page 90).

Portuguese gardens benefit enormously from the Atlantic climate. Although temperatures can reach 40 degrees at the height of summer – and sometimes stay there for six weeks at a time – high annual rainfall and generous supplies of natural spring

LEFT A view through the garden to the side of Casa de Serralves, built for Carlos Alberto Cabral, Count of Vizela, in 1935. When it was built, the house was in open countryside. From the 1940s onwards, however, the wealthier residents of Porto began to move out of the centre of the city towards the sea, and the neighbourhood changed dramatically.

RIGHT Luigi Manini brought teams of expert sculptors and stonemasons from Coimbra to realise his elaborate neo-Manueline vision for Quinta da Regaleira in Sintra. The house stands on the edge of the site, next to the shady lane leading out of Sintra towards Colares. Manini designed the garden to span the hillside above the house. The house has little part to play in the overall design.

water produce gardens that are refreshingly and surprisingly lush. The Moorish water tanks and Italianate fountains that decorate so many Portuguese gardens are filled to the brim with clear, ice-cold spring water. Often, this water has been brought to the garden using the ancient Arabic system of *minas*, horizontal shafts driven into the rock of a hill or mountainside to collect a vein of water and carry it out. In the garden the water may still be distributed using the stone surface channels originally seen in Arabic gardens. The water tanks, which tend to be much larger in Portugal than the average garden pool, are another legacy left by the peninsula's Arabic settlers. They are often built directly over a spring. The water flows continuously into the base of the tank, filling it to the brim and creating a clear, still mirror arranged to throw off reflections of the house, a tile-clad pavilion or a majestic tree. These tanks created a focal point in the garden, a place for relaxation and contemplation, or livelier activities involving boats or fishing nets. Stone benches are sometimes set into the base of the wall and originally a shady pavilion would often stand beside the water, or on an island at the centre of the pool. These buildings were usually made from wood, and consequently they have not survived. Eighteenth-century palace gardens near Lisbon might contain a tile-lined canal that could be used for boating parties (see page 17). Once again, the pavilions built beside, or even over the water, have long since disappeared.

Abundant water and a mild climate create ideal conditions for citrus. Orange trees have been a vital element of the Portuguese garden ever since the country's Muslim settlers made medieval, Islamic gardens on Portuguese soil, filling the enclosed spaces

ABOVE *This magnificent stone water tank and pavilion are the only surviving elements of Quinta das Torres' baroque garden in Azeitão. Spring water flows into the tank through scalloped leaves in two corners, filling it to the brim before flowing out again through holes in the opposite corners. Shoals of fish speed through the sparkling water, past the tiny landing stage where the family boat used to be moored.*

RIGHT *Magnificent tile-clad and battlemented walls, granite sculptures and towering trees crowd the skyline in the garden of Casa dos Biscainhos in Braga. The house was originally built in the country. Visitors are only reminded by the distant sound of traffic that Braga has spread to embrace and enclose the site.*

with the orange trees and the lingering scent of their pale blossom. The climate permits both sweet and bitter oranges to be grown in open soil, and in the sixteenth century it became fashionable to incorporate an orange grove into the garden, separating the lines of trees with narrow channels of fast-flowing water. The Portuguese are sometimes credited with bringing the first sweet oranges to Europe from India or the Far East. Those in favour of this theory suggest that Vasco da Gama brought sweet orange seeds, or even a seedling home after his voyage around the Cape of Good Hope in 1497. The opposition point out that the Genoese had been trading with caravans from the Levant throughout the fifteenth century, and were just as likely to have introduced sweet oranges to Europe through Italy. Whatever the truth may be, sweet oranges were commonly known as 'Portugals' in the Mediterranean and Near East until the end of the nineteenth century, and venerable orange trees of both sweet and bitter varieties are grown singly and in orchards in gardens all over Portugal. From the eighteenth century the citrus orchard was traditionally enclosed by a box hedge, low and neatly clipped.

Azulejos – coloured tiles – are the most distinctive feature of Portuguese garden design. They are particularly important in the gardens of Lisbon and in the Alentejo region, where they are used to decorate walls, benches, water tanks, canals, steps,

balustrades and planting troughs, intensifying the effect of colour and light throughout the garden. Sometimes the tiles create complex, glowing patterns and sometimes they form large, figurative tableaux that depict biblical, mythological or historical events, or comic scenes in which animals, typically cats and monkeys, are depicted mimicking human behaviour. These tableaux added another layer of experience to the garden, providing entertainment and intellectual stimulation, and creating a vivid extension to the garden landscape.

Tiles were first introduced into Portugal from Spain at the end of the fifteenth century. This event, which was to have such a profound effect upon the character of the Portuguese garden, was the result of a journey made in 1498 by Dom Manuel I to southern Spain. The king visited several palaces and in every one he saw magnificent *azulejos* decorations. The experience inspired him to import tiles from Seville and use them to decorate his own palace – now the Palácio Nacional – in Sintra. The king's enthusiasm for *azulejos* triggered a fashion among the aristocracy and by the beginning of the sixteenth century, when the country's first golden age was already in full swing, huge numbers of brightly coloured tiles in geometric or botanical patterns began to be imported to Portugal from workshops in Seville. Gradually, the Portuguese developed their own workshops, although they always looked to Holland, Italy and England for new styles and techniques.

Both garden making and *azulejos* production suffered a simultaneous decline at the beginning of the nineteenth century, when the French invaded Portugal and

the entire royal court migrated to Brazil. Despite these events, this book does encompass gardens made in the nineteenth and twentieth centuries. Among them is Quinta da Regaleira, a massive house and garden made at the beginning of the twentieth century and realised on the back of a family fortune built upon Brazilian coffee and precious stones.

The book falls into two sections. The first focuses on gardens north of Coimbra and the Mondego river. The gardens in the second section lie to the south of Coimbra, with most of them clustered around Lisbon. This geographical division is mirrored by distinct differences in the scale, design and planting of the gardens. The gardens in the first section were built predominantly in areas where granite is the indigenous rock. Granite is a dense and unforgiving stone that makes hard work for sculptors. Consequently, sculpture and other stonework in northern gardens is relatively simple. Most of the gardens in the second section are built in areas where pale, pliable lime-stone is readily available, and this has resulted in some very flamboyant stonework. Garden designers in northern Portugal were greatly influenced by the baroque, while the Arabic tradition continued to exert more of a hold further south, and *azulejos* were used in greater abundance. Further contrasts between north and south will emerge, and it will soon be evident that Portugal offers an extraordinary variety of wonderful gardens, too often neglected by garden visitors.

GARDENS TO VISIT

The nearest major town or city is given in square brackets.
It is advisable to check opening times.

QUINTA DO ALÃO, strictly by appointment: Senhor Jacome de Vasconcelos,
Rua da Mainca 204, Leca do Balio, Porto [Porto]

QUINTA DA AVELEDA, Apartado 77, 4560 Penafiel. Tel 255 718 200;
Fax 255 711 139 [Porto]

QUINTA DOS AZULEJOS, by appointment: Ludovico Mendonça, Secretary General,
Colegio Manuel Bernardes, Quinta dos Azulejos, Paço do Lumiar - 1600-549,
Lisbon; colegio@cmb.pt [Lisbon]

QUINTA DA BACALHOA, by written appointment: Vila Fresca de Azeitão, Alentejo;
ana.paula.matos@sapo.pt [Setúbal]

MUSEU DOS BISCAINHOS, Rua dos Biscainhos, 4700 Braga, Minho.
Tel 253 204 650; Fax 253 214 658; mbiscainhos@ipmuseus.pt.
Tues–Sun 10am–12pm, 2pm–5.30pm [Braga]

BOM JESUS DO MONTE, Braga, Minho. Tel 253 67 66 36; open daily [Braga]

PALACE HOTEL BUSSACO, Luso, Beira Litoral. Tel 231 937 970; Fax 231 930 509;
bussaco@almeidahotels.com [Coimbra]

PAÇO DE CALHEIROS, Calheiros, 4990 575 Ponte de Lima, Minho. Tel 213 300 541;
Calheiros@solaresdeportugal.pt [Guimarães]

CASA DO CAMPO, by appointment: Maria Armanda Meireles Molares,
4890 Celorico de Basto, Douro. Tel 055 361 231 [Guimarães]

QUINTA DA CAPELA, Estrada Velha de Colares, 2710-502 Sintra, Estremadura.
Tel 219 290 170; Fax 219 292 425 [Lisbon]

JARDIM DO PAÇO CASTELO BRANCO, Rua Bartolomeu da Costa, Castelo Branco,
Beira Baixa. 9am–7pm [Castelo Branco]

REAL QUINTA DE CAXIAS, Estrada da Gibalta, Caxias (opposite the railway station);
10am–6pm [Lisbon]

JARDIM BOTÂNICO DA UNIVERSIDADE DE COIMBRA, Coimbra 3049, Beira Litoral.
Tel 239 855 233/10. April–Sept 9am–8pm; Oct–May 9am–5.30pm [Coimbra]

RUÍNAS DE CONÍMBRIGA, Conimbriga, Beira Litoral. Tel. 239 941 177.
March–Sept 9am–8pm; Oct–March 9am–6pm [Lisbon]

PALÁCIO FRONTEIRA, Largo São Domingos de Benfica 1, 1500-554 Lisbon.
Tel 217 782 023; Fax 217 784 962. Guided visits Mon–Sat: June–Sept 10.30am,
11.00am, 11.30am, 12.00am; Oct–May 11.00am, 12.00am; closed Sundays and
holidays [Lisbon]

CASA DA ÍNSUA, 3550 Penalva do Castelo, Beira Alta. Tel 232 642 222;
Fax 232 415 400; casadainsua@visabeiraturismo.pt [Viseu]

QUINTA DAS LÁGRIMAS, Rua António Gonçalves, P-3041-901 Coimbra,
 Beira Litoral (adjacent to Jardim Botânico). Tel 239 802 380;
 Fax 239 441 695 [Coimbra]

CASA DE MATEUS, 5000 Vila Real, Trás os Montes. Tel 259 323 121;
 Fax 259 326 553; casa.mateus@utad.pt. June–Sept 9am–7.30pm, October, March,
 April, May 9am–1pm, 2pm–6pm [Vila Real]

PARQUE DE MONSERRATE, 2710-405 Sintra, Estremadura.
 Open summer 10am–6pm, winter 10 am–5pm [Lisbon]

QUINTA DE MOURÃES, 4415-660 Lever, Douro. Tel 227 650 712; Fax 227 631 047;
 geral@quintademouraes.com [Porto]

PALÁCIO NACIONAL DE SINTRA (Palácio da Vila), Largo Rainha D. Amélia,
 2710 Sintra, Estremadura. Mon, Tues and Thurs–Sun 10am–5.30pm [Lisbon]

PALÁCIO DA PENA, Estrada da Pena, 2710-609 Sintra, Estremadura.
 Tel 219 105 340; Tues–Sun: mid-June–mid Sept 10am–7pm, mid-Sept–mid-June
 10am– 5.30pm [Lisbon]

CASA DA PERGOLA, Av Valbom 13, 2750-508 Cascais, Estremadura.
 Tel 214 840 040; Fax 214 834 791; pergolahouse@vizzavi.pt [Lisbon]

QUINTA DA PIEDADE, strictly by written appointment: Teresa Schönborn,
 Quinta da Piedade, Colares, Sintra, Estremadura; teresa@casacadaval.pt [Lisbon]

PALÁCIO DO MARQUÊS DE POMBAL, Largo Marquês de Pombal, 2780 Oeiras,
 Estremadura. Tel 214 408 552. Summer 8am–8pm, winter 9am–6pm [Lisbon]

PALÁCIO DE QUELUZ, Largo do Palácio, 2745-191 Queluz, Estremadura.
 Tel 214 350 039, Fax 214 352 575. 10am–5pm Wed–Mon [Lisbon]

QUINTA DA REGALEIRA, Rua Barbosa do Bocage, Sintra, Estremadura.
 Tel: information 219 106 656; reservation 219 106 650;
 regaleira@mail.telepac.pt. Nov–Jan 10am–5.30pm, Feb–April 10am–6.30pm,
 May–Sept 10am– 8pm, October 10am– 6.30pm [Lisbon]

CASA DE SANTAR, by appointment: 3520 Nelas, Beira Alta. Tel 253 565 337;
 Fax 253 565 889; cortesdabeirasantar@sapo.pt or casasantar@santar-sa.pt [Viseu]

PAÇO DE SÃO CIPRIANO, by appointment, 4835-461 Tabuadelo, Minho.
 Tel 253 565 337; Fax 253 565 889; info@pacoscipriano.com [Guimarães]

SERRALVES MUSEUM OF CONTEMPORARY ART, Rue D. Castro 210, Porto;
 serralves@serralves.pt; Tues– Sun 10am–7pm [Porto]

PALÁCIO DE SETEAIS, Rua Barbosa do Bocage 10, Seteais, Sintra, Estremadura.
 Tel 219 233 200; Fax 219 234 277; htpseteais@tivolihotels.com [Lisbon]

ESTALAGEM QUINTA DAS TORRES, Vila Fresca de Azeitao 925, Alentejo.
 Tel 012 180 001; Fax 012 190 607 [Setúbal]

Eucalyptus trees reach great heights in Portugal's mild climate.

The Gardens
of Porto and Northern Portugal

The gardens in this section of the book lie north of Coimbra and the Mondego river, in the Beira Alta region, the Douro Valley, the Minho, and the city of Porto. Many of them belong to farmhouses. They are small, family gardens, and looking for them will lead you away from the main road, drawing you down narrow country lanes through a landscape that is lush, rural and often hilly and heavily wooded. With the exception of the Douro Valley, where the roots of vines nestle against warm, moist, slate bedrock, granite is the indigenous stone of these regions, and it is used in the garden to make the rounded coping on the edge of water tanks, the simple bowls of fountains, planting troughs, gate piers, finials and the 'chatting' seats so often set in companionable pairs into the garden wall. The hard, resistant quality of the granite defined the nature of these features, which are simply rendered, in a robust style with the minimum of decorative detail.

In the Minho the roads are lined with modest, domestic gardens. Most of them have a vine-covered pergola that is supported by granite pillars. The grapes on the pergola are used to make *vinho verde*, the local wine, and in the dappled shade beneath them flowers and vegetables grow side by side. No garden is without cabbages, the essential ingredient of *caldo verde*, a soup that forms the traditional introduction to every meal. Anywhere north of Coimbra is maize-growing country. Wooden maize-drying sheds supported, once again, by granite columns are a common sight in the fields. They are handsome, distinctive buildings, and sometimes they find their way into the design of a garden. The Quinta de Mourães in the Douro valley has an informal, modern garden with a fine maize shed in it (see pages 22, 26).

The majority of gardens in the regions covered by this section of the book date from the eighteenth century, although Jacques Gréber's twentieth-century design for the Parque de Serralves is one notable exception (see page 90). In Porto and the surrounding area the eighteenth century was dominated by the architecture of Niccolò Nasoni, the Italian architect responsible for introducing the baroque to Portuguese soil. Nasoni's arrival in 1725 coincided with new prosperity in Porto generated by the port-wine trade with England. At first Nasoni's practice was confined to the city, where he designed a number of palaces and churches in a rich and intense baroque

The mock battlements of Casa da Ínsua can just be seen through the leaves of a venerable Magnolia denudata *that has thrived against the back wall of the garden since 1842. The tree doubles as a hanging display of the orchids that the gardener cultivates in the pots suspended from its branches.*

style that determined the character of architecture all over northern Portugal. From 1735 he began to take commissions for *quintas* and their gardens on the edge of Porto. Nasoni popularised the Italianate concept of the villa garden in Portugal, furnishing it with statues, fountains and belvederes. The fountains took the form of baroque statues, an Italian idea that the Portuguese embraced wholeheartedly. Statue fountains soon became an essential element of the eighteenth-century garden, and even found their way into the *azulejos* tradition, becoming a standard image in the decoration of eighteenth-century tiles.

Several of Nasoni's gardens have been destroyed. Many of them may have perished in March 1809, when Porto was attacked by Napoleonic troops. The French occupation lasted less than a month but it was extraordinarily destructive. An English officer wrote the following account after returning to the house where he had stayed in 1808:

the fine balustrades [were] broken; the chandeliers and mirrors were shattered to pieces ... the choice pictures were defaced, and the walls more resembled a French barracks than the abode of a Portuguese *fidalgo* [nobleman] from the obscene paintings that were daubed on them. The beautiful garden was entirely ransacked; the charming walks and fragrant bowers torn up and demolished; the fountains broken to pieces.

BELOW LEFT *A stone window set into the old garden wall now frames a view of the new arboretum at Quinta do Alão, near Porto.*

BELOW RIGHT *An ornamental maize shed towers over the modern garden of Quinta de Mourães, a small hotel overlooking the Douro Valley.*

RIGHT *View across the Lima valley from the garden of Paço de Calheiros.*

Nevertheless, Nasoni's work survives in the gardens of Quinta do Alão (see page 30) and both the palace and the garden of Casa de Mateus (see page 72), which has a magnificent example of the double, balustraded staircase that Nasoni is said to have introduced into Portugal for the first time (see over).

The gardens of Northern and central Portugal benefit from a super-temperate climate with high summer temperatures, mild winters and rainfall throughout the year. These conditions create very lush vegetation and stimulate extraordinarily rapid growth in both plants and trees. Orange trees – a vital element of gardens all over the north – thrive in such gentle and generous conditions. Some parts of the Douro region are protected from the influence of the Atlantic by the Marão mountain range and the gardens in these areas benefit from a Mediterranean climate. From the sixteenth century onwards Portuguese gardens were enriched by exotic trees and plants brought back by merchants and explorers. These tender specimens acclimatised well,

and consequently the gardens encompass a varied palate of species from all over the world. The climate suited Australian plants particularly well, a fact that has had an enormous impact on the wider landscape. The hills of central and northern Portugal were originally clothed in North Atlantic pine and holm oak, but over the last forty years native species have been largely eradicated and replaced with Australian eucalyptus. The trees are cropped every seven years and will regrow naturally three times before they need to be replanted. The pulp is sold to the paper industry and brings good returns. However, the oily wood is highly flammable and fires sweep through the forests each summer, exposing the heat-blackened rocks of the hills, consuming leaves and bark, but sparing the twisted skeletons of the trees, which will often regenerate. In the garden the eucalyptus has received very different treatment. It has been grown as a specimen tree since the nineteenth century, and in gardens such as Casa da Ínsua (see page 66) and Quinta da Aveleda (see page 36), the fine eucalyptus trees have achieved an extraordinary height and girth.

One of the country's most important botanic gardens is attached to the University of Coimbra. It was founded in 1772 by the Marquis of Pombal as part of his modernisation of the entire education system. The garden was designed as an outdoor classroom and a science laboratory where medical students and botanists could learn from first-hand observation. However, it is also conceived as a highly ornamental space, with fountains, statues and handsome wrought-iron gates. The plant collection grew steadily, first to encompass tropical plants, then Australian trees and shrubs, and then, in the nineteenth century, trees from South Africa, South America and California.

Porto and the surrounding region have the highest general standard of horticulture in the country. French horticultural practices were adopted in Portugal during the nineteenth century, and in the Porto area ornamental gardening became an integral part of local culture. Several gardens contain camellias, many of them

The still, dark surface of this vast water tank was designed to reflect the extraordinary façade of Casa de Mateus. Niccolò Nasoni, an Italian baroque architect working in Portugal, is generally thought to be the designer of both the interior and exterior of the house. His work here was more fanciful and flamboyant than anything to be found in eighteenth-century Italy.

hundreds of years old. Camellias are winter flowering, but the variation in the flowering times of different varieties means that a garden can be refulgent with flowers from November to March. The flowers are particularly striking when seen against the camellia topiary that is such an important element of these gardens.

The history of Portugal's camellias is poorly documented. Portuguese sailors were the first Europeans to reach Japan, and it is sometimes assumed that they brought Japanese camellias into Europe for the first time. For many years there was a rumour that the ancient camellias in the garden of Casa dos Condes de Campo Belo in Vila Nova de Gaia had been there since the mid-sixteenth century. This story can be traced back to an unfortunate misunderstanding between the Count of Campo Belo and Dr Frederick G. Meyer of the United States Department of Agriculture. In 1959 Dr Meyer wrote an article saying that the Count of Campo Belo had told him that the *C. japonica* growing in his garden had been planted in the mid-sixteenth century.

LEFT *The gardens of Quinta de Mourães cover 6 acres (2.5 hectares). A small lake is home to swans, and rhododendrons, azaleas and camellias are given free rein to thrive in the acid soil.*

ABOVE *One of the many varieties of Anthurium growing in the greenhouses of the Coimbra botanical garden. Their unmistakable heart-shaped flower bracts earn them the popular name of 'painter's palette'. The bract surrounds the true flower – a colourful spike (or spathe).*

He went on to say, 'This is not impossible, since early Portuguese traders to the Orient first made contact with Japan in 1542. The discovery of these aged specimens extends the date of introduction of the Camellia back nearly 200 years, to about 1550.' Bold words that were hotly denied by another camellia expert, the late Robert M. Gimson. Meyer had interviewed the count in English. After a conversation in Portuguese, Gimson was able to clarify the situation: '... The Conde himself told me that Dr Meyer had misunderstood; he did not tell Dr Meyer the Camellias were 400 years old, but that documents substantiate that the manor and its garden were in the possession of his ancestors 400 years ago.'

Meyer's mistake – which must terrify anyone engaged in research – reopened the debate about the age of Portugal's camellias. Portuguese merchants in China and Japan were intent on filling the hold of their ships with valuable cargo. Why should they waste time gathering camellia seeds? If some eccentric sailor brought a pocketful of seed home with him, how could it possibly be viable after a long journey through humid, tropical air and freezing Atlantic storms? Who would attempt to keep a camellia plant alive on a ship where fresh water was often so scarce that the sailors had not enough to drink? No, there is nothing to validate the idea of sixteenth-century camellias in Portugal, but as the owners of the country's oldest plants appear to have a collective fear of scientific testing that might damage the plants, the unfortunate myth lives on, nurtured by the rapid growth rate and extraordinary size of the plants in northern-Portuguese gardens.

The first camellia successfully cultivated in Europe is generally believed to have been English, not Portuguese. It was imported from China by Lord Petre of Thorndon Hall in Essex, where it was reported to be flowering in 1739. The plant's single red flowers were much fêted and painted, and it was not long before camellia cultivation became highly fashionable in England. The golden age of the camellia came later to Portugal, where it began in 1800, and lasted until about 1900. According to an article written by José Marques Loureiro, the owner of Porto's most important camellia nursery in the second half of the nineteenth century, the first camellias reached Portugal between 1800 and 1810, where they were grown by a Mr Van-Zeller in his garden at Fiães in Vila Nova de Gaia. Loureiro was described by one of his contemporaries as 'a wholehearted amateur, endowed with an unquenchable love for camellias'. José Duarte Oliveira, writing in *Journal de Horticultura Prática* in 1871, went on to explain that Loureiro '... devoted himself for a very long time to their cultivation, and little by little he has made a collection of all kinds, so that today he unquestionably possesses the best collection in Portugal'. By 1884 Loureiro was offering 868 different varieties for sale at his nursery in Porto.

Between 1850 and 1900 all the best families in Porto and Vila Nova de Gaia met for camellia shows. Their passion had long since leeched out from Porto to the surrounding countryside, and in 1852 the anonymous English author of *Hints to Travellers in Portugal, In Search of the Beautiful and the Grand. With an itinerary of some of the most interesting parts of that remarkable country*, noticed camellias, 'of every kind and great size in the north (some being 25 feet high, with branches covering a circuit of 50 feet)'. It is clear from this account that the camellias had grown extraordinarily rapidly in the Portuguese climate. With these growth rates pruning soon became necessary. This was the origin of the wonderful *casa do fresco*, the camellia shade house that is so characteristic of gardens in the north of the country. The plants are pruned each year after flowering and trained to create magnificent green structures that serve as shady garden rooms in summer, and are studded with beautiful flowers in the winter and early spring. Sometimes they have a roof, doors and windows, and sometimes the plants are trained to form a huge umbrella. The venerable camellias of Casa do Campo create some of the most impressive camellia structures in the country (see page 60).

Camellias were also cultivated by the English families that settled in great numbers in Porto and the Douro Valley on account of the port-wine trade. By the end of the eighteenth century the port business was so profitable that one merchant, a Mr Harris, was able to commission Humphry Repton himself to design the garden on his estate at Gondomar. In England the fashionable camellia was only cultivated under glass, and expatriate gardeners revelled in Portugal's extraordinary growing conditions, filling the gardens of their beautiful *quintas*, town houses and summer houses with camellias and watching them thrive in Portugal's mild climate. Did the British expatriates share their passion for camellias with the Portuguese? If Charles Sellars' late-nineteenth-century description of the English 'Oporto families' is to be trusted, it seems unlikely:

> [They] have the air of owning the city, so Britanically, so unconsciously arrogantly, they walk its mountainy streets, play cricket and football in their own playing grounds, have rowing regattas on the river, meet for business and entertainment in their magnificent, eighteenth-century, granite Factory House, conduct their business across the Douro in their ancient and beautiful wine lodges, and superintend the vintage from their quintas far up the river. ... They have their summer houses and bathing beaches, their own society, entertainment, sports and church parade ... they have lived for centuries a jolly, self-contained British life.

RIGHT *Camellias flowering on colossal plants in the gardens of Casa do Campo. The garden has been cultivated by the same family ever since the camellias were planted at the beginning of the nineteenth century, but no record of the names of the original plants has survived.*

QUINTA DO ALÃO

Quinta do Alão is a lush, tranquil refuge in Porto's ever-expanding hinterland of roads and factories. You may catch a first glimpse of it as you hurtle, propelled by teeming traffic, down the main road. It rises from the fields like a *hortus conclusus*, a serene oasis entirely surrounded by high stone walls. The garden is entered through a long pergola supported by granite pillars and encrusted with the knotted stems of an ancient wisteria. High metal gates at its far end conceal a wide sandy courtyard that is flanked by the house and the family chapel. The garden is finally reached through a dim passage and a sturdy, bolted, wooden door. With each stage of this journey the silence and the sense of isolation from the outside world deepen. In this respect, Quinta do Alão is reminiscent of the intimate private garden spaces of the Moorish tradition.

The heavy wooden door opens directly onto the lowest level of the garden. Although there are records of a house built on this site by the Knights of Malta in the fifteenth century, the garden dates only from 1684. Quinta do Alão, originally known as Casa de Recarei, was home to a foster sister of Dom João IV during the seventeenth century, and it may be that the garden was built during this glamorous period in the *quinta's* history. Some of the finest trees in the garden – among them a magnificent *Magnolia grandiflora* – are said to date from this period. During the eighteenth century Niccolò Nasoni, the Italian architect whose designs for gardens and palaces had taken Porto by storm, was called in to refurbish Alão in his own highly fashionable version of Italian baroque style.

The garden is a crowded, intimate, beautifully maintained space. It consists of three shallow terraces furnished with simple, granite benches, pools, planting troughs, pergolas covered in

The eighteenth-century box parterres are packed with colourful flowers throughout the year.

wisteria and roses, and a magnificent array of ancient trees and shrubs. A narrow stone channel of clear, fast-flowing water divides the lower garden in two, evoking, once again, a memory of the Moorish tradition. This water channel and the garden pools are fed by an abundant supply of natural spring water. A pleasing jigsaw of geometric parterre beds on the central terrace was planted in the eighteenth century. The beds are enclosed by double box hedges, and in spring they are packed with flowering bulbs that give way in summer to annuals, so that there is no pause in the colourful succession. The camellias growing at the centre of the garden are very old. Time and careful pruning have combined to produce contorted structures of sturdy, gnarled boughs that reach a height of at least 30 feet (10 metres). The camellias blossom in February, and by the time they finish in March, the roses have already started to flower. Tree ferns, planted only fifteen years ago, also occupy this central space, thriving in temperatures that never dip below zero, even in the depths of winter.

When Niccolò Nasoni was invited to refurbish the garden in the mid-eighteenth century he worked principally on the uppermost terrace. Nasoni may have been trained in Tuscany, but he broadened his style to encompass elements of strictly Portuguese garden design, with all the exotic Moorish elements that this implied. Granite pavilions with ornate Moorish rooflines mark the corners of the upper terrace. On the stone wall behind them Nasoni designed a fountain that is the baroque version of an Arabic *chafariz* or wall fountain. The fountain is set into a towering, false façade topped with an elaborate skyline that is decorated with granite obelisks. The wall between the top of the façade and the fountain itself is entirely covered by the tightly-packed, dark green leaves of *Ficus pumila*. Into this dense mat of leaves a sharp scrolled line has been cut.

LEFT *Rose and wisteria pergolas are used to mark the garden boundary.*

ABOVE *Niccolò Nasoni's eighteenth-century additions bring an exotic atmosphere to the upper garden.*

RIGHT *The interlocking parterres are best seen from the raised terrace that spans the garden façade of the house.*

Within the line the stone is absolutely bare, creating an intense and dramatic contrast that can only be preserved by continuous maintenance. This exacting level of maintenance is typical. Ever since Senhor Francisco Jerome de Vasconcelos bought Quinta do Alão forty years ago he has worked in the garden himself, lovingly caring for what was already there and developing an entirely new area as an arboretum. He employs three gardeners and takes on extra help in the spring. The place glows with well-being.

The handsome granite water tank on the upper terrace is another of Nasoni's eighteenth-century contributions. A fountain at its centre is decorated with a coat of arms that incorporates the head of a dog. This is a visual reference to the title of the *quinta*. The word 'Alão' derives from 'alano', the name of a ferocious breed of dog that trotted into Portugal in 409 at the heels of fierce barbarian invaders called the Alani. It was a fighting dog, a hunting dog with the courage to herd cattle or face up to wild boar in the woods. Something huge and boisterous lives in a pen in the outer courtyard at Quinta do Alão. When it breaks out, as it invariably does shortly after the arrival of visitors, Senhor Vasconcelos struggles to restrain it, before introducing it as the more genteel ancestor of the alanos that gave his house their name.

Fifteen years ago Senhor Vasconcelos embarked on planting an entirely new section of the garden beyond the boundary wall. He has made a rich and wonderfully varied collection of specimen trees from all over the world, planting them in enclosures of clipped box. In northern Portugal's generous climate the trees have already reached an impressive height, and put on girth to match. They represent the third chapter in Quinta do Alão's rich history.

QUINTA DA AVELEDA

Should you drive towards Quinta da Aveleda in September you will have to join a convoy of small tractors hauling huge loads of grapes towards the farm for pressing. Progress is slow, but the vineyards and orchards to either side of the road are drenched in golden light and the air is warm and sweet. Eventually you will reach the yard and the convoy will fragment, releasing you at last. However, as you walk around the *quinta's* enchanting, romantic, woodland garden you will not forget for a moment that it is part of a very busy and successful working farm. The house and garden are set against a background of vineyards, pasture, handsome barns, cowsheds and wine cellars. The estate, which is the biggest in northern Portugal, has belonged for 300 years to the Guedes family, and they are the largest producers of *vinho verde* in the country.

Aveleda's garden was planted in the mid-nineteenth century by Dom Manuel Pedro Guedes, who also rebuilt and extended the seventeenth-century house. There is a stark and delightful contrast between the sun-filled, busy farmyard and the deep shady gully that forms the entrance to the garden. The sunken path is flanked by ferns and towering trees. The damp air carries a rich cargo of mossy, leafy scents. It is as if you had been suddenly transported from Portugal to a garden in Cornwall, or on the west coast of Ireland. Guedes and his designer (name unknown) have you reaching for your dictionary of garden history. The main part of the garden is planted with trees, rather in the style described by William Robinson in *The Wild Garden* (published in 1870). Oaks have been allowed to grow tall and to create a dense canopy. Rhododendrons, hydrangeas, camellias and azaleas thrive in their dappled shade. Between the oaks Guedes planted a number of interesting specimen trees –

Quinta da Aveleda and João da Silva's 'Four Seasons' fountain.

Birds and animals are well provided for at Aveleda.

among them *Aesculus indica* (Indian horsechestnut), *Liliodendron tulipifera* (tulip tree), *Cryptomeria japonica* (Japanese cedar), *Eucalyptus gunii* and *Platanus occidentalis* (American sycamore). The ground beneath the trees is covered in a dense mat of creeping ivies and periwinkles. Aveleda is well provided with water by underground springs, and when José Marques Loureiro described the garden in an article written for *Journal de Horticultura Prática* and published in 1882 many of the trees had already reached colossal heights. He was particularly impressed by a vast tulip tree, and a 'magnificent specimen of *Dasylirium longifolium*'.

A series of straight, tree-lined avenues divide the woods into separate areas, but between them are much narrower, winding paths leading to a series of follies that would sit well alongside Shirley Hibberd's mid-Victorian, *Rustic Adornments for Homes of Taste* (published 1856). The first of these is a fanciful cottage that serves as a gatehouse, complete with uniformed gatekeeper. It stands at the end of the avenue that links the *quinta* to the road and also forms the backbone of the layout. The gatehouse has a thatched roof and a comical thatched belfry. Branches have been used to clad the walls and support the tiny porch. From his miniature window the gatekeeper can look across the avenue and into the woods, where the azaleas flare into colour each spring. If he looks out through the door he will meet the benign gaze of the cows that are housed in barns on the opposite side of the road. Their milk is used to make Aveleda's famous cheese.

The cattle may be firmly excluded, but it was fashionable in the nineteenth century to keep smaller domestic animals and birds in ornamental houses in the garden. The Aveleda goat house takes the form of a circular stone tower with a spiral ramp around its outer wall. One of the delights of visiting nineteenth-century gardens in Portugal is that so much of the original furnishing remains intact. In this case it is the circular *faux bois* fence around the goat pen that draws the eye. Some

LEFT *Tastings of Aveleda's famous* vinho verde *take place on this decorative balcony overlooking the vineyards.*

RIGHT *A nineteenth-century wall fountain made for the garden by a local craftsman.*

of the goats stick their noses between the beautifully wrought twigs, others trot happily up and down the ramp, leaving the kids asleep in a nest of hay on the ground floor. Some years ago a veteran billy found himself ousted from power by a younger and more handsome rival. He is said to have expressed his despair by jumping to his death from the top floor of the tower.

Below the goat tower there is a long tree-lined pool punctuated by three islands. On the first is an ornate stone window salvaged from the house in Porto where Henry the Navigator is said to have been born. Stone scrolls and arabesques have been softened by centuries of erosion. The second island is little more than a rock with a powerful fountain on it, but the third is occupied by a magnificent, thatched tea house with branch-clad walls. Inside, the walls and ceiling are decorated with wonderful terracotta figures of aquatic creatures, including a frog, a crocodile, an alligator and a turtle. The tea table at the centre of the room is fashioned from coiled rope and has a wooden anchor as its base. A dusty bench against the wall is made in the shape of a boat, with oars as its back.

Beyond the pond the path leads out of the trees to a lush lawn that has been the scene of many family weddings and celebrations. Steps lead up from the grass to a paved terrace backed by an elaborate nineteenth-century wall fountain. Water flows from the leering mask at the centre of the fountain into a stone bowl, overflowing once again into zigzag channels that run between the paving slabs. The stonework is softened by *impatiens* rooted between the slabs, pots of flowers arranged on the steps, and the banks of variegated hydrangea to either side of the fountain.

The house, large and creeper-clad, stands at the lowest level of the garden. In front of it is a fountain known as 'The Four Seasons'. It was carved in the nineteenth century by João da Silva, who used portraits of the four Guedes sisters to decorate the shaft and represent the seasons. Behind the house and the small, seventeenth-century chapel is another pond, this time with a goose house at its centre that is built to resemble a thatched, fairytale cottage with a witch perched on its roof. This is the final absurdity in this captivatingly light-hearted garden.

CASA DOS BISCAINHOS

The curators of the Biscainhos museum in Braga do not permit their visitors access to the enchanting eighteenth-century garden until they have followed the prescribed route through the palace. This is no hardship. Palace and garden are intimately connected, and together they create a vivid impression of the lives of eighteenth-century *fidalgos*, or noblemen. The rooms are furnished with richly carved Indo-Portuguese furniture, and the garden is surrounded by high walls, some of them adorned with mock fortifications and sentry boxes. During the eighteenth century the lives of Portuguese women were still shaped by rules of enclosure inherited from the Arabic tradition. The *fidalgas* of Casa dos Biscainhos lived in utter seclusion in the house and the walled garden. In one of the rooms of the palace there is a dais covered in thick oriental carpets and scattered with cushions. This was where they sat, keeping a discreet distance from the men and surrounding themselves with daughters, female friends and maids. When the Duchess d'Abrantès came to Portugal in 1805 she was deeply shocked by many aspects of life in the court of Dom João, and was particularly catty about the practice of sitting on the floor:

> When I entered the Princess of Brazil's drawing room all the *dames of honour* were seated – guess, reader, where? On the floor! Yes! On the floor! With their legs crossed under them, like tailors, or rather like Arabs, who have bequeathed this among the many other customs they have left to the Peninsula.

The main façade of Casa dos Biscainhos dates from the seventeenth century, but the garden was built in the mid-eighteenth century, when Braga was at the forefront of rococo

The garden façade of Casa dos Biscainhos in Braga.

style, and home to the country's most distinguished granite sculptors. This happy combination produced a garden that is delightfully light-hearted and flamboyant. It is built on three levels. The first is a flower garden that lies directly behind the palace and is defined by low granite walls punctuated by decorative wrought-iron gates. The walls rise sharply in a series of pleasing curves and scrolls to meet the gate piers. One of the gates is flanked by double piers capped with obelisks that are set at a rakish angle to the wall. The other is topped by seated *putti* blowing hunting horns, their chubby legs dangling. The piers are magnificent, sculptural objects, and their decorative effect is intensified further by a facing of tiles. The use of *azulejos* in the gardens of northern Portugal was generally restrained, but here yellow, white and blue patterned tiles cover

LEFT *One of a pair of* putti *that flank the gate of the main garden.*

RIGHT *The mock fortifications of the garden wall can just be seen beyond the cupola of the nymphaeum at the bottom of the garden.*

the gate piers, the garden walls and the domed roof of the two-storey pavilion on the edge of the flower garden, intensifying the effects of light and colour. The walls incorporate the planting troughs that are so typical of the Portuguese garden, and marigolds and bright geraniums trail down over the glistening tiles. In places the troughs give way to pairs of stone seats set into the thickness of the wall. Once again, these *alegretes* were a highly traditional feature of the eighteenth-century garden. Elsewhere, the garden is densely furnished with statues and fountains, all of them dextrously carved from granite in a capricious rococo style.

Inside the perimeter wall, the upper garden is wonderfully crowded. Much of the space is occupied by box parterres. The Portuguese traditionally created very complex designs with box and Biscainhos is no exception. The curvaceous, interlocking patterns of parterres like this one are said to have been inspired by the Arabic decorative tradition. Inside their neatly clipped hedges the parterre beds are planted with roses and a rainbow selection of flourishing annuals. Water for the garden's flowers and numerous fountains comes from the ancient spring of St Gerald that rises beyond the garden wall, by the Church of the Misericórdia. Miraculous powers have always been attributed to St Gerald's water, but it is probably the combination of irrigation and horticultural expertise that makes this garden glow with well-being. During the 1960s thousands of Braga's men left the town and travelled to France in search of employment. Gardening both public spaces – such as the Jardim de Santa Barbara – and private gardens fell into the hands of women, and there it has remained. The town's public spaces, gardens and parks are unusually pretty and well maintained, and they blaze with colour in spring and summer.

At Biscainhos the camellia cool houses, or *casas do fresco*, are both the garden's greatest feature and the gardeners' greatest

LEFT *It is unusual to find* azulejos *used with such abandon in a northern-Portuguese garden.*

RIGHT *Flowers and* azulejos *combine to bring colour to Biscainhos throughout the year.*

challenge. The camellias were originally planted against a wooden framework and trained to form circular rooms and shady green roofs. The *casas do fresco* are immense, they tower over the garden, their leaves shining in the sun. In the heat of the summer they provide dense, effective shade. Russell Page visited Biscainhos in 1935, and this may have been the inspiration for his comment on arbours in *The Education of a Gardener*:

> Arbours cut from yew or laurel are not usually places where one likes to linger. The only arbours I have ever enjoyed were flowery ones in Portugal. There in many eighteenth-century gardens regular summer houses are shaped entirely in huge old camellias which still, after centuries of clipping, are set solid in February and March with their bright rosettes of scarlet, pink and white.

By the end of March the ladders and scaffolding have been erected, and the gardeners have embarked on a skilled and painstaking annual pruning.

When Page visited Biscainhos the area below the flower garden was still occupied by an orange grove where rows of vegetables grew between the trees. He found white peacocks in the elegant, balustraded enclosure at the garden's lowest level. The palace and garden had belonged to the Nespereira family for hundreds of years, but when the family sold them to the town council in 1963 Biscainhos became a museum, and the fruit and vegetable garden became redundant. Today the vegetables are gone and only a few venerable orange trees huddle below the retaining wall of the upper garden, their sweet fruit lying untouched on the ground. However, there is nothing poignant or nostalgic about this happy, thriving place.

BOM JESUS DO MONTE

This massive staircase and the twin towers of the church at its summit dominate the view to the east of Braga. It might be surprising to find a penitential staircase in a book about gardens, but Bom Jesus do Monte is an extraordinary piece of eighteenth-century landscape architecture, and a showcase for some magnificent box and camellia topiary. The staircase, which was commissioned in 1722 by Dom Rodrigo de Moura Teles to celebrate his investiture as Archbishop of Braga, was designed as an approach to the ancient hilltop shrine of Bom Jesus. By 1725 the first section was finished. The Archbishop died in 1728 and the project was eventually completed by Carlos Amarante between 1784 and 1811. Amarante was one of the finest architects in northern Portugal at this time, and he also rebuilt the crumbling shrine, transforming it into a monumental, neo-classical church.

The first section of the *escadaria*, or staircase, consists of steep steps that zig-zag up the hill. The climb is not for the frail or faint-hearted, and ever since 1882 there has been a water-powered funicular railway to transport pilgrims directly from the base of the staircase to the church at the top. Passengers save their knees, but they miss the extraordinary experience of toiling up the steps and pausing to gaze into the dimly-lit interior of the chapels that mark the fourteen stations of the cross. Each one contains a carved and painted *mise-en-scène* of almost life-size figures that re-enact the agonising journey. Candles placed by passing pilgrims faintly illuminate the interiors of some chapels. In others the brightly painted figures glow in the dusky light.

The second section of the staircase is steeper, but much less solemn. The granite walls are whitewashed, and on a sunny day the effect is quite dazzling. The approach to this section

The sanctuary church of Bom Jesus do Monte seen above the penitential staircase.

LEFT *Camellias grow in the small enclosed garden spaces to either side of the staircase.*

ABOVE *Statues of biblical figures combine with box and camellia topiary to crowd the skyline above the staircase.*

of the *escadaria* is flanked by fanciful granite pillars that are encircled by narrow watercourses. Water driven up through the core of the pillars emerges at the top and speeds down the watercourses in a shining, twisted ribbon. Water is never lacking in the gardens of northern Portugal, and here it adds an extra dimension, bringing the staircase to life with sound and light. As you look up towards the church, the view is entirely filled by the eternal criss-crossing of the stairs and the serried ranks of plump topiary shapes cut from camellia and box. This section of the ascent is dedicated to the five senses and they are represented by a series of delightful wall fountains. Statues

of biblical figures mark the end of each terrace. Some of them sport elaborate beards, others wear cloaks or turbans, creating an increasingly exotic and rococo impression at each level of the stairs. The fountain on the first landing is dedicated to Sight and the fountain figure has water gushing, somewhat shockingly, from iron pipes that emerge from its eyes. It is flanked by eagles – proverbially sharp sighted - and topped by a statue of a man rubbing his eyes. The second fountain represents Hearing, and by now you should be used to the sculptor's rather literal interpretation of his brief. Water is in copious supply, and here it pours from the ears of the fountain figure. Carved oxen, with their large and perpetually twitching ears, stand to either side. The fountain is crowned with the figure of a musician. Pausing only to drag your hand through the cool water in the bowl, you must toil onwards and upwards. On the next landing you will find Scent, and you may find the effect

of water streaming from the fountain figure's nose disturbing. Long-muzzled hounds flank the fountain and a perfumier towers above it. Each landing is paved with black and white mosaic, and now you stand in front of Taste to watch the water pour from its mouth. The statue above holds food and drink on a tray and the fountain is flanked by monkeys. This is said to be a reference to a traditional method of finding water in Africa. Monkeys were fed large quantities of salt before being let loose to slake their thirst, their masters in hot pursuit. The fountain on the final landing is dedicated to Touch. Water pours from an urn grasped by a pair of hands. Below it a spider catches a fly, and the statue above is without a sword – a reference to the *touché* in a sword fight.

It's not over yet, but if your legs are aching consider the pilgrims who make this ascent on their knees. Bom Jesus is a tourist attraction, but it is also a pilgrimage site, and on every fountain of the staircase little candles gutter in the damp air. The final stage of the staircase is dedicated to the three cardinal virtues. On the first landing there is a statue of Faith with her eyes covered. To the left there is a tiny nursery selling azaleas, camellias and pot plants. Hope occupies the second landing, and on the third there is a mother holding two babies to represent Charity. The wide terrace at the top of the steps was the original site of the shrine of Bom Jesus do Monte. Now it is a wide and blessedly flat terrace with a wall fountain representing a pelican nurturing two babies on its own blood. The grassy slopes above it are planted with elaborate *broderie* parterres.

The early-twentieth-century Romantic park that covers the hillside above the church is imprinted with the happiness of generations of families on sunny, Sunday afternoon outings. There is a magnificent concrete grotto containing a clear pool that teems with fish. Concrete stalactites drip from the ceiling. A circular belvedere further up the hill is supported on pillars made from *faux bois*, a clever composite of wood and stone invented by the French in the eighteenth century. At the top of the hill brightly painted rowing boats jostle at the edge of a pretty boating lake.

FAR LEFT *Sight is one of the five senses represented by statues on the staircase.*

CENTRE LEFT Faux bois *twigs cover the ceiling of the circular belvedere above the church.*

LEFT *Pebble mosaics decorate the staircase at ground level.*

RIGHT *A flowering camellia seen against the bare branches of winter trees beside the staircase.*

The water staircase cuts through the woods and reaches its dramatic conclusion at the garden's lowest level.

MATA DO BUSSACO

Nothing could prepare the visitor for the shock of a first encounter with the extravagant architecture of Bussaco and the mysterious walled landscape that surrounds it. The palace and the ornamental garden beside it were the last additions to a landscape that has been continuously inhabited for more than a thousand years. The first layer of Bussaco's history was laid down in the sixth century, when hermits chose it as their home and built their huts among the trees. This tradition continued, unbroken until 1628, when it was formalised by the Carmelites who made it into their first 'desert', the spiritual retreats created for brothers who felt called to imitate the austere and isolated lives of the early Christian fathers. Over the years twenty-two of these retreats were founded all over Europe. The forest was an essential part of their layout.

At Bussaco the brothers built the monastery at the centre of the forest and it still stands there today, immediately beside the palace. They also constructed an enormous wall to enclose the 260-acre (105-hectare) forest and decorated parts of it with elaborate mosaics made from local stone. In 1642 Pope Urban VIII recognised the importance of the site by issuing a papal bull that threatened to excommunicate anyone found felling a tree without express permission from the prior. At this stage there was only one opening in the forest wall, the Coimbra Gate. The words of Urban VIII's bull were inscribed above it, where they can still be seen today. An additional threat came in the form of Pope Gregory XV's bull of 1622. Once again the words are inscribed at the entrance, and their purpose is very plain. Any women found inside the gate would suffer immediate excommunication. The forest had become an enormous cloister. Today it is a popular tourist attraction, but it still retains something of the atmosphere of a *hortus conclusus*, sacred and enclosed.

In 1689 Joseph Pitton de Tournefort, the French botanist, visited Bussaco and made a survey of its trees. *Eléments de botanique, ou Méthode pour reconnaître les Plantes* was published in 1694, and in it de Tournefort listed some of the trees that he had seen at Bussaco. All of them were native to Portugal except for a Central American cypress (*Cupressus lusitanica*). There is no archival evidence to confirm its provenance, but the tree is

LEFT *A glimpse of palm trees in the neat parterre garden behind the palace.*

RIGHT *The fabulously complex neo-Manueline carving of the ground-floor loggia was entirely designed by Luigi Manini.*

said to have been planted in 1648. Some people believe that this was the first time that a Mexican cypress had been cultivated in Europe. Others point out that Saint John of the Cross – a Spanish Carmelite – had already planted a *C. lusitanica* during the sixteenth century, in the monastic garden of El Carmen de los Martires in Granada, and it is quite possible that seeds were sent to Bussaco by Spanish Carmelites. Whatever the truth may be, it is remarkable to find a monstrously tall, seventeenth-century tree still thriving in Bussaco's forest.

The forest's wooded slopes are covered in a web of winding paths. Several of them lead to chapels that were built among the trees by different patrons over the centuries. There is also

a *Via Sacra*, a steep penitential walk commissioned at the end of the seventeenth century by João Melo, Bishop of Coimbra. It links the monastery to the *Cruz Alta*, a stone crucifix on top of the hill, and is lined with chapels that mark the fourteen Stations of the Cross. Christ's final journey is re-enacted inside the buildings by powerful life-size, terracotta figures.

The papal bulls of the seventeenth century held fast, protecting the forest from intrusion and allowing the monks to continue their devout, cloistered existence inside its wall for hundreds of years. In 1810, however, disaster struck and Bussaco was sucked into the Peninsular Wars. As General Massena led Napoleon's troops along the Viseu road towards Coimbra, the Duke of Wellington decided to station 51,000 Anglo-Portuguese troops and 60 cannon along Bussaco's forested ridge. Sixty-five thousand French troops took up their positions on the hills opposite the ridge. Wellington made the monastery his headquarters. Every room was occupied, except for the prior's and that of a monk who had cunningly filled his cell with furniture. Wellington was victorious, but the Battle of Bussaco was the beginning of the end of monastic life in the forest. In 1834 the new Liberal government decreed the extinction of all monasteries and convents and confiscated their possessions. The forest fell silent, empty of monks or holy men for the first time in 1,300 years.

Another layer was added to Bussaco's landscape in the mid-nineteenth century, when it became the property of the state and the forest was developed as an arboretum containing trees from Australia, the Far East, Africa and America. Towards the end of the century Queen Maria Pia, wife of King Luis I, commissioned Marcellino and Giuseppe Roda, landscape architects from Piedmont in Italy, to prepare a scheme for a complete transformation of the park. The two brothers drew up plans for numerous rustic buildings, bridges, stepping stones, aviaries and aquariums, rose gardens and orchards. They eventually focused their attention on the Fonte Fria, a natural

spring that they remodelled to create a dramatic water staircase. Water was made to run down 144 steps before flowing into a naturalistic pool. Water from the pool then flowed down into the Valley of the Ferns, another feature from this era, where Australian tree ferns still thrive in the humid air.

In 1888 Bussaco's history took another turn when Emidio Navarro, minister of public works, hit on the idea of building Portugal's first grand railway hotel at Bussaco. He invited Luigi Manini, a celebrated Italian set designer working at the Royal Opera House in Lisbon, to produce a plan. Manini seemed to have no difficulty in making the leap from the fantasy of

LEFT *Many of Bussaco's ancient trees have reached colossal heights. They thrive on a combination of downpours like this one, and considerable heat.*

ABOVE *The mysterious atmosphere of the forest is never more apparent than on a foggy day.*

his richly evocative stage sets to the reality of bricks and mortar. In 1888 he made a number of large, 'scenographic sketches'. The building that he created in these beautiful watercolour sketches was as whimsical as anything that you could expect to see on set. The images were handed over to a group of engineers capable of attending to the practicalities of building the massive structure, with all its decorative towers, spires, battlements, exterior staircases, gargoyles, terraces and loggias. When it came to detailed decoration, however, Manini had to be called back in to provide the drawings for window and door frames, gargoyles, balustrades and carved friezes. Today the palace is encrusted with Manini's breathtakingly complex version of neo-Manueline decoration. Behind the palace there is a colourful and beautifully maintained parterre garden, a long reflecting pool and a series of raised pergolas and arbours. These features are all contemporary with the hotel, which was completed at the beginning of the twentieth century.

CASA DO CAMPO

Casa do Campo combines in a very small space all the most appealing elements of the northern-Portuguese garden. It has a copious supply of cool, clear water, a wonderful display of ancient camellias, a solid backbone of neat box hedges and a fine array of granite tanks, water channels, fountains and benches. The rambling seventeenth-century house has belonged to the Meireles family ever since it was built. On one side it is flanked by a tiny baroque chapel, and on the other by one of the most delightful gardens of the region. Narrow, balustraded, stone bridges link chapel and garden to the reception rooms on the first floor of the house.

In central and southern Portugal gardens often follow the Moorish tradition; they are enclosed, private spaces, cut off from the outside world by high walls. By contrast, gardens in rural areas of northern Portugal are frequently designed to take full advantage of the view. At Casa do Campo the garden is elevated to the same level as the first floor of the house. From the far end there are long views across the Tâmega valley to the mountains. Visitors arrive in the courtyard at ground-floor level and look up at the low, whitewashed walls of the garden, and at the weird camellia topiary spilling over them. Casa do Campo's camellias were planted early in Portugal's golden age of camellia cultivation, a craze that endured for the whole of the nineteenth century. The first plants reached Portugal from England between 1800 and 1810. According to an article written by José Marques Loureiro in his own *Journal de Horticultura Prática* (vol. 13, 1882), they were ordered by a Mr Van-Zeller of Porto from the Mile End Nursery in London, and also by other amateur camellia growers, many of whom 'occupied high positions in the Custom-House of Oporto'.

Flowers appear on Casa do Campo's ancient camellias to mark the beginning of the new year.

TOP LEFT *Vast, barrel-shaped camellias flank the main entrance to the garden.*

ABOVE LEFT *A towering rhododendron blooms as the camellias' flowering comes to an end.*

TOP RIGHT *Pots of colourful flowers decorate the garden wall.*

ABOVE RIGHT *The side of one of Casa do Campo's famous camellia shade houses.*

RIGHT *Looking through the door of the shade house towards the garden boundary.*

The warm damp climate of northern Portugal proved to be perfect for camellia cultivation, and the plants grew at a spectacular rate. The creation of extraordinary camellia topiary of the kind seen at Casa do Campo was the imaginative outcome of the practical necessity of keeping the camellias under control. The treatment of the plants here is more elaborate than in any other garden in the country. Two immensely tall camellia cylinders flank the gate, and beyond them the path is lined by asymmetrical camellia umbrellas of an astonishing height. The centre of the garden is marked by a circular, granite pool full of clear water that is piped to the garden from a hillside spring some two miles (three kilometres) away. Stone channels carry the water to every corner of the garden. The pool is surrounded by a circular camellia screen about 20 feet (6 metres) high. Arches cut into the screen frame views of the garden in all directions. Beyond the pool is one of the two square *casas do fresco*, shade houses constructed entirely from clipped camellias. This is camellia architecture at its most impressive. Both buildings have solid dark green walls and high pitched roofs. The plants bloom throughout March, their flowers studding the sheer sides and sloping roofs. Hand pruning begins in June and takes up to two months to complete. The double box hedges that enclose the parterre beds are pruned with electric clippers.

Casa do Campo is a friendly, family garden, where flowers and vegetables grow side by side. The bizarre camellia structures are underpinned by a more formal design of box hedges that surround beds filled with the evergreen variety of agapanthus (*Agapanthus praecox*). In early summer the dark hedges seem to enclose pools of bright blue water.

LEFT *The triangular form of the oldest camellia in the garden can be seen at the far end of the wall. It has been painstakingly clipped by hand every year since the beginning of the nineteenth century.*

CASA DA ÍNSUA

To reach many of Portugal's finest gardens you must leave the main roads and take narrow, deserted lanes past fields and forgotten villages. This is one of the great joys of garden visiting, and Casa da Ínsua provides a wonderful excuse to drive deep into the Beira Alta, with its hazelnut groves and orchards of figs, apples and pears, and the vineyards that produce grapes for the wine of the Dão region. Casa da Ínsua stands on the edge of the tiny village of Penalva do Castelo, at the heart of a large estate belonging to the Albuquerque family. A high wall and wrought-iron gates with ornate stone piers mark the boundary of the land. The wall encloses a 100 acre (40 hectare) estate, where a network of private carriage drives were built in the mid-eighteenth century and then lined with trees. A letter written by Manuel de Albuquerque in 1909 describes an avenue of oaks, one of palms, another of Mexican cedars from Bussaco (see page 54) and a box tunnel that ran for about 1000 feet (300 metres). Four hundred Italian cypresses were planted along the boundary of the estate, and some still stand there to this day.

Casa da Ínsua was built by Luís de Albuquerque de Mello Pereira in about 1780. *Casa* means house, but this modest title does not describe the rural palace that Albuquerque built from family wealth combined with the profits of the time that he spent as governor of Mato Grosso in Brazil. The pale, pretty façade of the house is enlivened by elaborately carved window cases. Two pavilions flank the main body of the building, breaking up the roofline and adding an exotic flavour with their mock battlements and wrought-iron balconies. Manuel de Albuquerque's description of the garden that lies below this lovely facade is still valid today:

The complex forms of the parterre beds at Casa da Ínsua are overlaid with flowers.

LEFT *This camellia in the garden of Casa da Ínsua begins flowering in October.*

RIGHT *Several box-lined beds were set aside for vegetables and cutting flowers.*

BELOW RIGHT *The garden seen from the first-floor loggia of the house.*

The garden has a geometric design ... All the beds are surrounded by box hedges in the shape of cornucopiae, vases, fans etc ... It is curious to think that this box has been clipped with every possible care ever since it was planted.

He goes on to say that the garden had been beautifully maintained by three generations of gardeners who were all from the same family.

The design of Casa da Ínsua's parterres is extraordinarily elaborate, even by Portuguese standards. In addition to the forms described in Albuquerque's letter, there are numerous curved and apparently amorphous shapes that nevertheless interlock to create a wonderful green jigsaw. It is never possible to get an overview of this complex design because of the vast, mushroom-shaped camellia shade houses and high hedges that spring up among the parterres, and the circular camellia hedge at the centre of the garden.

Flowers are an immensely important aspect of the Portuguese garden, and Casa da Ínsua blazes with colour throughout the year. Bougainvillea, morning glory and Cape honeysuckle flower in their own seasons against the walls of the house. The camellias in the garden are studded with flowers in January and February. The *Magnolia denudata* that has grown against the back wall of the garden since 1842 bears its pale flowers in spring, and during the summer the parterre beds are filled with a succession of pink roses, orange canna and pale shasta daisies that give way to different varieties of sage, zinnia and marigold later in the year. During the summer the hexagonal pool inside the camellia 'room' at the centre of the garden is also filled by the pink flowers of *Nelumbo nucifera*. Next to the house there is a long, oblong water tank where a single swan swims. It is built against a wall covered in morning glory.

By the end of the eighteenth century it was fashionable in northern Portugal to plant a wood as part of the garden. At Casa da Ínsua trees were planted beside the house, among them some cedars of Lebanon and sequoias that survive to this day. At the beginning of the twentieth century the Italian architect Nicola Bigaglia was commissioned to renovate and enlarge this woodland area. Bigaglia planted more trees, creating numerous glades where he built fountains, seats and a small pool with an island.

LEFT *Many generations of gardeners have used this tile-clad fountain to fill their watering cans.*

RIGHT *The garden was designed to be seen from the pretty first-floor loggia of the house.*

Stars, circles, anchors, triangles, scrolls and lozenges combine in the parterre beds on the upper terrace.

CASA DE MATEUS

They never made rosé on the Casa de Mateus estate, but the façade of the house has adorned Mateus rosé bottles for decades. Niccolò Nasoni (see page 21) is generally held to be the architect of both the interior and the exterior of the central block, although the wings to either side of it are thought to be part of an earlier building. He was probably commissioned some time between 1730 and 1743 by António José Botelho Mourão, third Morgado of Mateus. This is Nasoni unleashed. The still, dark surface of the huge water tank in front of the house reflects a building more intricate and inventive than anything made during even the most flamboyant of Italy's high baroque moments. The front door is on the first floor and a double balustraded staircase links it to the paved courtyard below. The double staircase was a familiar feature in the Italian garden from the mid-sixteenth century, but when Nasoni brought it to eighteenth-century Portugal it was a revolutionary innovation. The family coat of arms rises triumphant above the door and the casements to either side of it are decorated with a medley of fleurs-de-lis, shells and wheat sheaves. The roofline is offset by wonderful sculpted figures that hold metal spears and wear plumed hats and formal eighteenth-century clothes. To flank them Nasoni designed an array of soaring pinnacles that also serve a more practical purpose as chimneys.

The garden that lies behind this building is an equally powerful celebration of the baroque. To reach it you must walk down a passage that passes beneath the centre of the double staircase and emerges on the other side of the house into a bright space that is confined by the house on one side and the pale walls of the chapel on the other. Portugal has absorbed successive waves of exotic influence and the terrace is covered

by complex box parterres that seem to combine the richly ornamental traditions of both Islamic and Indian art. The hedges
are planted to form stars, anchors, circles, lozenges, triangles,
scrolls and a medley of other complex shapes. Many of the
beds are surrounded by a double hedge, the inner one much
lower than the outer. Some of these hedges enclose more box
figures set into gravel, others create a margin for beds of colourful annuals or roses, and in some crape myrtles (*Lagerstroemia
indica*) burst into flower each September. A shady grove of
camellias shields the entrance to the cypress tunnel, one of
the most impressive features of this most impressive garden.
The tunnel is 60 feet (18 metres) high. A massive, curved ladder
used at pruning time enables the gardeners to reach the apex
of this smooth, green, cypress mountain. Bare branches in
the dimly-lit interior create a gaunt, gothic nave. Beyond it,

a vine-covered pergola supported on sturdy granite obelisks
leads out into the sunny fields.

The cypress tunnel links the upper and lower terraces of
the garden. The three spring-water pools to the left of it were
a happy twentieth-century addition and are best appreciated
from below. The parterre garden to the right is enclosed on
one side by the great bulk of the tunnel itself, and on another
by a magnificent undulating hedge. The space is filled with a
complex pattern of interlocking parterre beds planted, once
again, with crape myrtle and a colourful mixture of flowering
plants. In the garden beyond, low box hedges embroider the
gravel with extraordinary arabesques and curlicues, crowns and
fleurs-de-lis. A second vine-covered pergola with granite pillars
runs along the base of the retaining wall. L. F. de Tollenare,
a French cotton merchant who visited Porto and the Douro

LEFT *The broad path separating
the orchards and vegetable plots on
the side of the house.*

ABOVE RIGHT *The flamboyant
flourishes and arabesques of the
broderie parterre on the lower
terrace.*

BELOW RIGHT *The windows
on the side of the house, overlooking
the orchard and a few surviving
fruit trees.*

valley in 1817, commented on the number of grape pergolas that he saw in the local gardens:

> The main decorative feature consists of well-cared-for pergolas which are placed on the terraces facing the sea, the Douro river or else some beautiful valley. These pergolas are useful as they simultaneously provide wine and permit one to stroll in the shade. They are held up by granite prisms, whose six faces are parallelograms and which are shaped with such skill that it excites my curiosity, since it must be difficult to raise these pillars without breaking them, as they are pieces of granite four inches thick and they are frequently fifteen to eighteen feet in height.

The pillars of the pergolas at Casa de Mateus are very much more robust that those seen by de Tollenare, but they are carved into prisms with flat faces just as he describes. The more

slender granite pillars are still used to support grapes in the fields all over northern Portugal.

Orchards and vegetable plots were a vital component of Portugal's eighteenth-century gardens. Box hedges were generally used to enclose the area and give it structure. This practical part of the garden always seems to have been the first to perish. At Biscainhos for example, the box enclosures remain, but inside there is nothing but a few sweet orange trees. At Casa da Santar the hedges are intact once again, but inside them there is only grass.

The orchard and vegetable garden of Casa de Mateus ran the length of the house, and there is still a large and very decorative irrigation tank at one end of the space. The structure of the garden – a long path flanked by hedges and spanned by handsome topiary arches and a series of box 'rooms' – is intact. Several old fruit trees remain, and the stone guttering used for irrigation is still set into the grass.

FAR LEFT *The side of the monumental cypress tunnel in the lower garden.*

LEFT *Dramatically scalloped hedges divide the lower garden into two parts.*

RIGHT *The geometric parterre beds of the lower garden lie fallow in winter, but in spring and summer they blaze with colourful flowers.*

Neat parterres and tightly clipped topiary contrast with wilder forms in the camellia grove beyond the garden.

CASA DE SANTAR

The Counts of Santar have been making wine in the Dão region since 1640. The core of Casa de Santar was built by them at the beginning of the seventeenth century, and the house has been lived in by thirteen generations of the family. It has an elegant first-floor loggia and a tiled roof with upturned corners in the Pombaline style and ornate chimney pots. These features give the house a slightly exotic air that is compounded by the *azulejos* surrounding the doors and windows, and the lemon trees that have been trained to grow against the walls. The Countess of Santar currently lives there, and her son, Pedro de Vasconcellos e Souza, is the winemaker on the family's very successful estate.

The garden was originally laid out in the eighteenth century and restored at the beginning of the twentieth. A path flanked by broad hedges and tall box pyramids divides the upper terrace which is overlooked by the first-floor loggia of the house. The space to each side of it is crammed with circular and lozenge-shaped beds that are surrounded by low box hedges and packed with floribunda roses. Statues, towering topiary obelisks and neat cones punctuate the layout, creating a delightfully crowded view in all directions. The two terraces below the main garden were originally used for growing fruit and vegetables. The area is still enclosed by box hedges, as was customary in the eighteenth century, but now there is nothing inside them but grass. A pool at the lowest level is a useful source of water for irrigation. There is an abundant supply of water at Casa de Santar. One of the curiosities of the house is the seventeenth-century kitchen, where spring water flows continuously into a stone tank. William Beckford saw a similar arrangement in the kitchen of a monastery near Lisbon:

ABOVE LEFT *The windows of the house are surrounded by colourful* azulejos *decorations.*

BELOW LEFT *The entrance to the seventeenth-century family chapel, which is dedicated to St Francis.*

ABOVE *The horse fountain stands beside the old stable block. It is decorated with* azulejos *designed by José Maria Pereira Cão.*

LEFT *Detail from the twentieth-century* azulejos *panels decorating the horse fountain.*

LEFT *Roses grow in lozenge shaped box parterres.*

BELOW LEFT *The garden is designed to be seen from the balcony and the handsome granite loggia of the house.*

RIGHT *A view across the garden, towards the chapel and its bell tower.*

Through the centre of the immense and nobly groined hall, not less than sixty feet in diameter, ran a brisk rivulet of the clearest water, flowing through pierced wooden reservoirs, containing every sort and size of the finest river fish.

The estate makes 1.5 million litres of wine each year which are exported to eighteen different countries, and all of the outbuildings are used for this purpose. However, there used to be a stable block at the bottom of the garden, and a fountain beside it where the horses were taken to drink. The horse fountain is a highly decorative drinking trough fed by spring water that pours from a grotesque mask on the wall behind it. The *azulejos* on each side of the mask are inscribed with the date 1790. This was probably the date when the original trough was built, but the tiles that decorate it today were produced during the restoration of the garden in the early twentieth century. The originals were designed by José Maria Pereira Cão, a distinguished tilemaker who was also employed by Dom Carlos I to restore the tiles on the boating canal in the gardens of Queluz. Taking inspiration from the lake house at Palácio de Fronteira (see page 134), he decorated the panels to either side of the central fountain with prancing horsemen. The horses and the figures of their riders are identical in each panel, but each face is the portrait of a different member of the Santar family.

The broad camellia hedge creates a dense, gleaming boundary between Paço de São Cipriano and the fields beyond the garden.

PAÇO DE SÃO CIPRIANO

I n northern Portugal *paço* is used as an abbreviation of *palácio* or palace. Paço de São Cipriano is not palatial in the usual sense, being neither vast in scale, nor formal in design. It is a dearly loved farmhouse, a beautiful building on an estate that has belonged to the same family since the fifteenth century. The house stands beside the pilgrim route to Santiago de Compostela, and for many centuries it has served as a hostel for pilgrims and other travellers, a tradition that continues to this day. Despite the illusion created by the first-floor loggia and the huge tower emerging from the roof, this is not an ancient building. The original, fifteenth-century house burnt down at the beginning of the twentieth century. This new house was built after the fire to a design conceived by the owner and an Italian architect. It is thought that much of the garden dates from the same period.

The beauty of Paço de São Cipriano depends upon the three traditional elements of the northern Portuguese garden: copious supplies of clear spring water, carved granite and crisp, camellia topiary. It is a compact, family garden, much loved by Senhor Sottomayor, the current owner, and his wife and daughters. The main axis is a broad path flanked by neatly clipped hedges and topiary buttresses. It leads from the front of the house to a semicircular granite water tank built against the side of the hill. The still surface of the water throws back reflections of the statue in a small nymphaeum, the coloured-pebble mosaic surrounding it, and the trees in the forest beyond the boundary wall. Fields and woods enclose the garden on all sides, and these glimpses of open countryside add greatly to the charm of the place.

Tall hedges conceal the gardens to either side of the path, creating a couple of garden rooms. The left-hand side is planted

ABOVE *View across the garden from the first-floor loggia.*

RIGHT *The camellias at Paço de São Cipriano flower from January to April.*

LEFT *Huge topiary forms dwarf benches set beneath the hedge.*

BELOW *The garden's main axis is stopped by an oval pool that was probably built at the beginning of the twentieth century.*

with elaborate arabesques of clipped box. The ancient azalea that towers over these parterres is covered in flowers each spring. In June the perimeter hedges are lined by agapanthus, densely planted and the deepest blue. A little summer house made from the finely-carved fragments of a much older building stands on the edge of the garden. Beside it a beautiful tiled seat stands against the boundary wall. The yellow and blue tiles are decorated to a seventeenth-century design, suggesting that the seat was part of a much earlier garden layout. The square granite tank also pre-dates the existing garden. Water from a hillside spring is funnelled into the tank through a lion mask inscribed with the date 1810. The water that fills the tank to the brim is sparklingly clean and icy cold. The right hand garden is enclosed on two sides by a towering camellia hedge that is studded with flowers from January to April each year. It is so wide that a small arched exedra has been carved out of it. The hedge is carefully pruned immediately after flowering each year, and like everything else in this charming place, it thrives on a diet of abundant water and lavish care.

ABOVE *The house, with its mock-medieval tower, and the chapel glimpsed through trees on the right-hand side of the picture.*

LEFT *Spring water pours off the hill into a square tank set against the boundary wall of the garden.*

RIGHT *This statue stands above the pool at the end of the garden's main axis.*

A view of the side of Casa de Serralves and the green garden beneath it.

PARQUE DE SERRALVES

Casa de Serralves is surrounded by the only important private garden to be made in Portugal during the first half of the twentieth century. The house was built in 1935 for Carlos Alberto Cabral, who bought the title of Count of Vizela when the monarchy was abolished in Portugal. There was already a nineteenth-century garden on the site, but in the modern part of the garden the paths are made from a pinkish-red soil that matches the walls of the house designed in the International style by José Marqûes da Silva, one of the country's leading architects at that time. The count commissioned Émile-Jacques Ruhlmann, the renowned French designer of interiors and furniture, to work on the flamboyantly art-deco interior of the house, and he looked to France once again for a landscape architect.

Jacques Gréber was selected to design the immediate surroundings of Casa de Serralves although he never visited the site in person. Gréber had graduated from the École des Beaux Arts in 1908 and departed two years later for America where he worked on numerous significant projects, both as an architect and an urban planner. In 1925 he designed the Jardin des Plantes in Paris and in 1937 he was appointed master architect of the Paris Exposition. He also worked on a number of private gardens in America and Europe. As a landscape architect, Gréber was influenced both by his own French tradition and by the Islamic gardens of Spain. The garden that he designed at Villa Reale, near Lucca in Italy, consists of a series of pools linked by narrow water channels and reflects this passion for Islamic garden design.

Casa de Serralves stands on a broad terrace. Gréber took his cue from the simple, unembellished lines of its façade.

LEFT AND ABOVE *Jacques Gréber made a strict division between the green garden around the house and the rose garden beyond it.*

He designed a series of shallow terraces flanked by trees. Down the centre of this vista he created a water staircase made up of rectangular pools linked by steps. The water, which emerges from a grotto beneath the upper terrace, flows down this staircase to a lotus shaped fountain at the lowest level. The design was a softened version of modernism. It was not very innovative in a European context, but in Portugal it was revolutionary. Gréber also planted a rose garden in traditional, box-lined beds. The raised rose pergola is built, like the house, from cast concrete.

The Serralves estate covers 45 acres (18 hectares) and incorporates woodland, meadows, lawns and formal gardens built during three distinct periods. During the 1930s Gréber also built an iris garden, a sunken tennis court and a curved wisteria pergola. Underlying these modern features are the remnants of the original nineteenth-century garden – a magnificent entrance avenue and a lake with a grotto and a wooded island at its centre. Beyond the lake there are greenhouses, stables and fields. After the count's death in 1968 the house was sold to an industrialist called Delfim Ferreira. In 1987 it was bought by the state and made into a museum. By 1999 the new Museum of Contemporary Art had been built to designs by Alvaro Siza. Much thought was given to the site of this exciting new building. Siza was told not to fell any mature trees, and he designed the new building to make as little impact on the existing landscape as possible. A 7.5 acre (3 hectare) area immediately around the museum was relandscaped, using indigenous plant species already found on site.

LEFT *Casa de Serralves was constructed in granite which was then overlaid with concrete details.*

BELOW *View towards the house, from the lotus shaped pool at the bottom of the garden.*

RIGHT *View from the house, down the stepped water channel to the lotus pool.*

THE GARDENS
OF LISBON AND CENTRAL
PORTUGAL

When the mid-nineteenth-century author William Butler wrote about Sintra in his book *The Tagus and the Tiber*, he said:

> It would be beautiful in any country, no wonder then that it is so much thought of in bare, unwooded, sunburnt Portugal. Around it you see nothing excepting the brown fields, without a tree or a blade.

Butler may have exaggerated the contrast between Sintra '...buried in foliage, rich in picturesque objects and surmounted by precipitous crags...' and the arid landscape around it, but it is true that the Portuguese climate becomes progressively hotter and drier from north to south. Sintra is the exception to the rule, and its distinctive microclimate is of great significance in this context because it encouraged the creation of some of the country's most important garden landscapes. The town has an extraordinarily humid and relatively cool climate. These conditions are the product of the *nortada*, the north wind that carries cloud inland from the Atlantic. The cloud gets trapped against the Serra de Sintra, the mountain ridge that rises dramatically from the coastal plain. Consequently, Sintra is often overcast until mid-morning, even at the height of summer, and the evenings can be misty and cool. On the southern slopes of the Serra these conditions create the subtropical growing conditions that produced the extraordinary garden of Monserrate (see page 138).

The city gardens of Lisbon feel the influence of both the Atlantic and the Mediterranean climate. Summers are hot, but sea winds bring some rainfall throughout the year. These conditions combined with the wealth of state and church during the eighteenth century to produce some of Portugal's largest and most magnificent gardens. The southernmost garden in the book is Quinta da Bacalhoa (see page 114) in the Alto Alentejo. In the Baixo Alentejo and the Algarve, however, water and wealth were both in short supply and the garden-making tradition did not penetrate.

The majority of gardens in Lisbon and central Portugal were built in the eighteenth or nineteenth centuries. However, the earliest garden builders were the Romans, who occupied Portugal from 210BC to the fourth century AD. A series of

Casa da Pergola stands in the centre of the busy seaside town of Cascais. It has belonged to the same family for over a century and today they run it as a small hotel. During the 1920s the white stucco walls of the nineteenth-century house were inset with colourful azulejos *panels and architraves.*

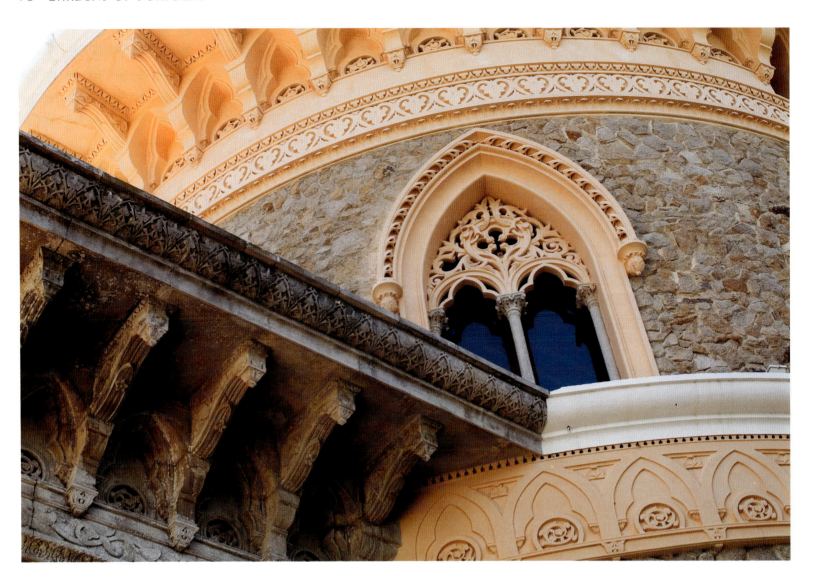

ABOVE *Monserrate, outside Sintra, has belonged to the Portuguese state since 1949. Recent restoration has revealed the full splendour of the nineteenth-century building designed in a Moorish-Gothic style by James Knowles for Sir Francis Cook. Cook was a collector, and the house was originally filled with antiques, paintings and oriental furniture.*

RIGHT *The classical Roman garden of the House of Water Jets in Conimbriga was originally surrounded by colonnades and an elaborate mosaic floor. The villa lay beyond the garden, and the main reception room opened onto its central axis. In spring the irises growing on six islands in the pool burst into flower, turning the water a new and darker shade of blue.*

ABOVE *Monserrate on its hilltop, glimpsed through palm fronds from the terrace of Quinta da Capela.*

ancient Roman gardens have been excavated in Conimbriga, an important town midway between Olissipo (Lisbon) and Bracara Augusta (Braga), and the courtyard garden of the villa known as the House of Water Jets has been reconstructed. Intricate mosaics cover the ground and the large pool at the centre of the space is surrounded by a colonnade. Six tiny islands with decoratively curved and indented edges emerge from the water in the pool. This is an unusual and intrinsically Portuguese element in an otherwise typically Roman layout. The islands are clothed in earth and packed with irises that flower in a purple haze each spring. Hundreds of low-level water jets play across the beds. Variations in this design were reproduced in various seventeenth- and eighteenth-century gardens (see, for example, pages 120 and 130).

History told through the medium of gardens can become a fragmented story. The departure of the Romans in the fourth century was followed by a lacuna filled only by the Moorish invasion of the eighth century. 'Moors' is a collective term used to describe the successive waves of Arab and Berber settlers in the Iberian peninsula. They were the architects of gardens with brimming water tanks and brilliantly coloured tiles, gardens full of the scent of citrus blossom and enclosed by high walls. These places survive only in literature, but something of their exotic atmosphere is preserved at the Palácio Nacional in Sintra. The palace was originally a Moorish

alcázar lived in by the governor of Sintra. After the reconquest it was converted into a palace for the Christian kings of Portugal. Dom João I had the existing building enlarged and restructured, but he chose to use a team of freed Moors as his workforce. Consequently, the Moorish character of the building was preserved. It became a palace fit for a Moorish caliph, a magnificent labyrinth of a building with an array of intimate garden spaces. There are loggias, balconies, an open-air, tile-clad audience room, and a series of garden courtyards furnished with tanks of cool, clear water.

ABOVE *The centre of Cascais is closed to traffic and Casa da Pergola stands on one of its busiest pedestrianized streets. Passers-by constantly stop to gaze at the colourful façade of the house and the garden, where curved* azulejos-*clad seats nestle among flowers growing in raised parterre beds. The intensely decorative style continues at ground level with complex pebble mosaics.*

In the largest of these, the Ladies Courtyard, water falls into a raised, narrow tank and throws flickering shadows through the long windows of the Room of the Swans. The windows of this beautiful room stretch down to the floor, and consequently people sitting on carpets and cushions inside could look out over the surface of the tank. A magnificent *casa do fresco*, or 'shade house', occupies the opposite wall. The camellia shade houses common to northern Portugal give way to these elaborate, grotto-like structures in the centre and south of the country. They are always cool, damp retreats, their walls decorated with shells, mosaics, shards of Chinese porcelain, glass, stones or *azulejos* in an infinite variety of combinations.

Most of the walls of the Palácio Nacional, both inside and out, are decorated with *azulejos*. In the garden courtyards tiles – many of them unusual relief tiles dating from the beginning of the sixteenth century – are used to decorate walls, planting troughs, the sides of water tanks, benches and staircases. Lisbon became the centre of Portuguese tile production, and gardens in and around the city have the finest examples of *azulejaria* in the country. In palace gardens built in the seventeenth century, like Palácio Fronteira (see page 130), or the eighteenth century, like Palácio de Queluz (see page 152), the tiles are used to create huge narrative tableaux. However, *azulejos* can also be used in more modest contexts, such as the garden of Casa da Pergola in the seaside resort of Cascais. Casa da Pergola was built in the nineteenth century. During the 1920s it was renovated and given the extraordinarily colourful facade that it has today. White walls combine with woodwork painted in an oriental shade of red. Polychrome tiles create frames for the doors and windows and bougainvillea clings to an ornate balcony on the first floor. This is a seaside house with a seaside garden, its colours bold and bright. The tile-work continues on curved stone seats set among the box-lined flower beds.

The tiles that the Portuguese garden inherited from the Islamic tradition tended to be used in enclosed and intimate garden spaces. Once again, the Portuguese were inspired by the ancient, Moorish tradition, and high walls continued to be built in central Portugal long after the Moors had been expelled. This tradition irritated Henri-Frédéric Link, a Frenchman visiting Lisbon at the end of the eighteenth century. 'It is most frustrating and annoying', he said, 'to ride around and face the risk of being lost for hours because of these high walls which do not permit anyone to enjoy the view.' The inside of the walls were covered in climbing plants, 'which they cover like a closely woven mesh', and to Link they seemed 'more the walls of fortresses than of gardens'. Link was undoubtedly biased by his irritating journey, but there is some truth in his image of the garden as an enclosed, fortress-like space. In the eighteenth century aristocratic women still lived the cloistered lifestyle instilled by

ABOVE *The dramatic view across the Serra de Sintra from the terrace of the Pena Palace. The palace and the naturalistic landscape surrounding it were built for Ferdinand Saxe-Coburg in the mid-nineteenth century.*

the Muslim tradition. They existed within a closed community made up of the family and the household servants, where the relationship between master and servant was very close. The Marquis of Fronteira described his family as consisting of '...my mother and my aunts, João Evangalista Machado, who exercises the functions of butler of the house, [and] Dona Mariana, my sister's chambermaid...'. The enclosed garden was an extension of this enclosed, nuclear structure, a sanctuary, concealed from the outside world, where the ladies of the family could take exercise in absolute privacy.

When William Beckford visited Portugal at the end of the eighteenth century, he also observed this continued Moorish influence, finding it even in the monastic gardens of San José, outside Lisbon:

We were shown by smiling friars into a small court with cloisters supported by low Tuscan columns. A fountain playing in the middle and sprinkling a profusion of gillyflowers gave an oriental air to this little court that pleased me exceedingly. The friars seem sensible of its merits and keep it tolerably clean. ... The friars would show me their flower garden, and a very pleasant terrace... neatly paved with chequered

Francis Cook gathered plants from botanic gardens in Rio de Janeiro, London and Lisbon to plant in his garden at Monserrate. He was particularly fond of evergreens, and the garden is full of palms, cypresses, pines and conifers. He worked alongside Francis Burt, head gardener, and together they divided the enormous site into areas devoted to plants from New Zealand, Australia, China, Japan, Mexico, Peru and Africa.

tiles interspersed with knots of carnations in a style I should conjecture as ancient as the dominion of the Moors in Portugal. Espaliers of citron and orange cover the walls and have almost got the better of some glaring shellwork with which a reverent father ten or twelve years ago was so idle to encrust them. Shiny beads, china plates and saucers turned inside out compose the chief ornaments of this decoration.

Trust Beckford to find fault, but his account does serve to draw our attention to this kind of enclosed, monastic garden space. In 1750, when 200,000 of Portugal's population of 3,000,000 lived in convents or monasteries, gardens of this sort must have been very common. However, the majority of them would have been lost during successive purges of the country's monastic orders. The attractive tradition, so despised by Beckford, of using *embrechados*, a combination of stones, pebbles, shells,

semi-precious stones and shards of glass and china, to create a shimmering mosaic on the walls of grottoes, cascades, fountains and terraces continued unabated until the nineteenth century. It was an extension of this taste for intricate decoration that made Indo-Portuguese inlaid furniture and exotic, hand-printed fabrics so popular inside the house.

Garden making reached a magnificent climax in Lisbon and its hinterland during the eighteenth century, but this was also the century of a devastating earthquake. On 1 November 1755 earthquake, fire and flood killed 30,000 people. The loss of human life was combined with the wholesale destruction of public and private archives, libraries, paintings and even currency. Gardens were caught up in this devastation. In Colares, near Sintra, for example, the Cadaval family's sixteenth-century Quinta da Capela and its walled garden were ruined. Only the chapel itself, perched high above house and garden, survived. In 1773 the *quinta* was rebuilt in a simple, rustic style and the garden was replanted with box hedges that divided the space into four large enclosures. Today the house is a tranquil hotel, the garden is virtually unchanged, although the fruit trees that probably filled the box enclosures are gone, and effective new planting has been added to the upper level, where ancient cork trees overhang a large tank brimming with water.

ABOVE *Casa da Capela, outside Sintra, is an eighteenth-century manor house that has been converted into a small hotel. The original building on the site was built in the sixteenth century by the Marquis of Cadaval, but it was badly damaged during the earthquake of 1755. The existing building and the simple garden surrounding it date from 1773. The current owners have created a new garden on a level with the eighteenth-century water tank above the house. Deep blue agapanthus crowd the beds in spring.*

RIGHT *The garden of Quinta da Piedade is made up of a series of 'rooms' laid out on the site of an abandoned lemon grove. It was designed by the Marchioness of Cadaval during the 1930s. She covered the walls and garden buildings with tableaux of rustic scenes made up from eighteenth-century tiles that she had rescued from derelict buildings.*

The Cadaval family originally owned most of the land on the western slopes of the Sintra mountains, overlooking Colares. Quinta da Capela was sold, but Quinta da Bela Vista and Quinta da Piedade still belong to the family. Piedade was the last house built in Colares by the Cadaval. It is a nineteenth-century building on the road to Monserrate with a small garden that hangs suspended above a beautiful view of open fields and undulating woodland. In 1935 Dom António Alves Pereira de Melo, the

These two reptilian creatures stand guard over the exit from a network of damp and highly atmospheric tunnels blasted from the hillside. They are carved from limestone, an easily worked stone which lent itself to the complex designs of Luigi Manini. Here, as so often in the garden, sophisticated limestone forms are set against a rustic granite wall.

Marquis of Cadaval, had the house restored and moved into it with his Venetian wife. The marchioness was a great art collector and, as founder of the Sintra Festival, she was queen of the Portuguese music scene. The garden that she created on the site of an abandoned citrus grove below the house was built around a large open-air concert hall that is still used today. To either side of it she made a series of charming rooms enclosed by low walls and hedges. The surfaces of the walls and garden buildings are entirely covered in eighteenth-century blue and white *azulejos* that she salvaged from derelict buildings, saving them from certain destruction.

Throughout the eighteenth century members of the royal family and their courtiers, politicians, cardinals and bishops commissioned gardens. After the earthquake of 1755 many aristocratic families decided to abandon Lisbon and move to their country estates outside the city. This promoted a new wave of garden building, and because many houses and gardens had been very neglected they required extensive restoration to bring them into line with contemporary fashion.

The nineteenth century saw the introduction of the naturalistic landscape to central Portugal. The first landscape to be planted in this style surrounded the Pena Palace in Sintra. William Baxter, an English visitor to Portugal in 1850–51, wrote a vivid description of the palace gardens, a 'charming paradise' that tumbled down the hillside, high above Sintra:

> A smooth carriage road, winding in graceful sweeps up the valley, leads to the principal entrance, the huge rocks, left as nature placed them, contrast beautifully with the flowers of the geranium groves, the bright arbutus berries, the green leaves of acacia and sensitive plant, and the bushy firs... Walks wind around the heights to various points of view, and stone benches, each one having a name, enable the visitor to enjoy at his leisure this charming paradise.

Granite is the indigenous rock of northern Portugal, but at Coimbra granite country gives way to a belt of fine, pale limestone. This geological change had an enormous impact on the character of gardens built in the centre of Portugal, where stone was highly worked to produce very complex sculptures and decorations. In the nineteenth century, when neo-Manueline style was the height of architectural fashion, stonemasons and sculptors working with limestone from Ançã and Portunhos were inspired to produce work of an extraordinary complexity. Some of the finest examples of this work can be seen in the gardens of Quinta da Regaleira (see opposite and page 160). The nineteenth century also saw the introduction of the English romantic and picturesque styles of gardening that were executed on a grand scale.

QUINTA DOS AZULEJOS

Quinta dos Azulejos is best visited at rush hour, when the traffic churning through the narrow lanes surrounding it will cause you maximum anxiety, and the workmen excavating the square outside will be using their drills to deafening effect. It is under these circumstances that you will best appreciate the garden as a sanctuary, a wonderful outdoor salon, cut off from the ugly realities of life beyond its high walls. The space is designed in the Mediterranean–Islamic tradition to be entirely inward looking. Who needs views when the garden's undulating walls, its elegant benches, urns, pillars and planting troughs are entirely covered in amusing *azulejos* decorations? Within the confines of this colourful, elegant space, the noise of traffic is drowned by the laughter and running footsteps of small children attending Colégio Manuel Bernardes, the school now housed in the *quinta*. The gardener pauses and looks up from his weeding to greet his favourites as they fly by.

Quinta dos Azulejos was built for António Colaço Torres. It was unusual, even in the mid-eighteenth-century, when *azulejaria* was achieving a wonderful climax in the Portuguese garden. It was so unusual that members of the royal family made a habit of travelling out of Lisbon between 1756 and 1760 to visit it. It was not the concentration of *azulejos* that drew them – they were used to tiles covering walls and other flat surfaces in the garden. Here, however, *azulejaria* went three dimensional, entirely clothing pillars, planting troughs, arches, benches and other sculptural and architectural surfaces. In places the tiles themselves imitate architectural features such as columns and cornices, and the effect of wood, marble and stucco. Their shining surfaces combined with elegant sculptures, fountains, grottos and an abundance of colourful and

A colonnade of tile-clad pillars leads to a naturalistic fountain made from tufa and embrechados.

ABOVE *Each of the curved
benches in the garden is decorated
with rustic scenes.*

RIGHT *The semicircular loggia
with its polychrome* azulejos
decorations.

highly scented flowers to create the uniquely intense and exuberant atmosphere that the royal family must have craved.

A pergola thickly clad in jasmine runs down the centre of the site. Today it is a thoroughfare that links the original *quinta* to a new school block. Eighteenth-century visitors had no such destination. They used the garden like an open-air drawing room, where they might link arms with a friend and wander along the broad paths beneath the perimeter wall. The path to each side of the entrance is lined with tile-clad pillars and benches that give formality to the space, creating the decorous atmosphere of the hall in a large house. The blue and white *azulejos* tableaux on the walls are surrounded by polychrome frames in the fanciful rococo style that followed the all-consuming craze for blue and white tiles in Portugal. The panels depict biblical scenes – the Marriage at Cana, the Feeding of the Five Thousand – alternating with *fêtes galantes*. In these tableaux the courting couples meet against a fascinating garden backdrop of parterres, fountains and towering terraces. Around the corner the mood changes abruptly to become deliberately burlesque. During the Enlightenment the garden was often the setting for menageries of strange or exotic animals that were earnestly studied at close quarters. On the west wall the panels appear to mock this worthy pursuit by depicting absurd animals corralled in a variety of unlikely combinations. In one tableau an ostrich is stooped upon by an eagle in an aviary that also contains a variety of parrots, a vulture and a macaw. Next door a baboon shares his accommodation with a herd of deer. Beside them a combination of ridiculous waterfowl process solemnly

around a fountain. Hidden among their ranks is a dog that walks pertly on its hind legs, imitating the storks on the other side of the pool. The final tableau shows monkeys as the unlikely companions of a lion and a bison. All the panels on this wall are painted in the aubergine tone obtained from manganese oxide. The planting troughs between the panels are filled with red geraniums and the benches crowded with pots of bright flowers. In spring the shady square beds between the wall and the central pergola are packed with pale arum lilies.

Three different workshops were engaged to produce the *azulejos* for the garden, and on the east wall the style changes once again. Here simple blue and white panels depict scenes from Ovid's *Metamorphoses*, always a popular theme in the garden. A deep tile-clad grotto stands against the end of the wall,

FAR LEFT *The tile panels on the west wall depict an ill-assorted mixture of exotic animals.*

ABOVE *The magnificent arch that shelters the grotto of Europa.*

topped by a flamboyant statue of Europa. The semicircular loggia opposite the grotto is the most elaborate structure in the garden. The pillars, the bench and the elegant seat backs are entirely covered in polychrome tiles. In spring the entire structure is swathed in jasmine that fills the air with its scent.

The garden that was created as a playground for the aristocracy has now become a children's playground. I hope that the gods and goddesses, the milkmaids and bumbling shepherds, the enraptured lovers and peculiar animals on the tiles enrich the dreams of the children that play there every day.

QUINTA DA BACALHOA

Every aspect of Quinta da Bacalhoa demands a superlative. The house is one of the finest early Renaissance buildings in Portugal, the tank and the pavilion beside it are the most beautiful structures of their kind, and among the tiles that decorate every surface, both inside and out, are some of the oldest *azulejos* in the country.

There have been buildings on this site in Azeitão since the fourteenth century, some of them quite splendid, but the existing *quinta* was constructed and the garden built when Brás de Albuquerque bought the estate in 1528. Brás was the illegitimate son of Portugal's great hero, Afonso de Albuquerque, who was viceroy of India and the effective founder of the country's eastern empire. An explanation for the Italianate design of the palace is easily uncovered in Brás de Albuquerque's biography. In 1521, a few years before buying the estate, he was chosen by Dom Manuel I to be part of the entourage that accompanied his daughter, Infanta Dona Beatriz, to Italy. The journey took Albuquerque to several Italian cities where he would have encountered the revolutionary architecture of the High Renaissance. The palace that he built around the remains of the existing buildings in Azeitão was a wonderful expression of this Italian experience. The L-shaped building encloses two sides of a compact parterre garden with a simple fountain at its centre. Box hedges surround the fountain, inscribing a complex pattern of interlocking arabesques. A high hedge encloses the garden on the third side, and an inventory of 1630 suggests that the space may originally have been entirely enclosed by a fourth wall. The loss of this wall has opened the garden up to the surrounding landscape, creating continuity between the different parts of the garden,

The parterre below the loggia of the Quinta da Bacalhoa. The area beyond it was originally planted as a citrus orchard.

and destroying the intrinsically Portuguese sense of enclosure. The inventory also describes citron and lemon trees growing against the garden walls. The house was built like any decent Italian *palazzo*, with a west-facing loggia on the first floor, and the parterre beds were designed to be seen from this vantage point. Dazzling, *azulejos* friezes decorate the inner walls of the loggia, their colours radiating across the garden.

Quinta da Bacalhao and its garden are an education in *azulejaria*, and the lesson starts on the raised walk that links the house to a magnificent water tank and the pavilion beside it. The brick walk is punctuated by tile-clad benches and planting troughs, enclosed on one side by the garden's boundary wall and on the other by a low tile-clad balustrade. These are all typical features of the gardens of central Portugal, but at Bacalhoa the tiles are unusually interesting. For decades Brás de Albuquerque imported *azulejos* from Mujédar workshops in Seville, and it is these early-sixteenth-century floral *azulejos* that decorate the balustrade. They were made by imprinting the soft clay with a negative image of the design, a system that

FAR LEFT *Aresta-work* azulejos *in the pavilion overlooking the water tank.*

BELOW LEFT *A detail of the* azulejos *inside the pavilion.*

LEFT AND BELOW *Maiolica tile panels inside the pavilion.*

EVPHRATES

created raised lines to keep the liquid glazes separate before firing. This relatively primitive technique is known as *aresta*. The low planting trough on the opposite side of the walk is decorated with *alicatados*. These are Mujédar tiles of a single colour, and here they are set in an egg and dart pattern that dates from the second half of the sixteenth century. The benches are covered with *azulejos* made with the maiolica technique introduced into Portugal from Italy in the middle of the sixteenth century. The wall above these colourful benches was originally decorated with ceramic *tondi* (or roundels) in the style of della Robbia. The original *tondi* were sold to Italian collectors at the beginning of the twentieth century, but they have since been replaced with copies.

The space immediately below the raised walk was once filled with 'infinite orange trees, lemon trees and citrons'. This description, made by Joaquim Rasteiro, dates from 1885, but the citrus grove was part of the original sixteenth-century layout. It was common from the sixteenth century onwards to incorporate an ornamental orchard of this kind into the garden. At Bacalhoa the venerable trees were grubbed out at the end of the twentieth century to make space for a vineyard. Sadly, numerous garden orchards have been lost. Stone irrigation channels set into the ground are often the only surviving trace of their existence.

The raised walk continues to hug the wall along two sides of the garden, but it is interrupted at its mid-point by a square tank and the Casa do Tanque – three beautiful pavilions linked by tiled loggias. The tank encloses a sheet of clear water that is big enough to row the boat moored at its edge, big enough to reflect the pale walls of the pavilions that rise out of it, and the tops of the trees beyond. The inside of the pavilions are decorated with a blazing display of *azulejos* in a mixture of *aresta* work and more modern maiolica. The introduction of the maiolica technique in the mid-sixteenth century revolutionised tile production. Suddenly it was possible to paint directly on to a tile, and as a result of this innovation the Portuguese developed a taste for large narrative tableaux of *azulejos* in the

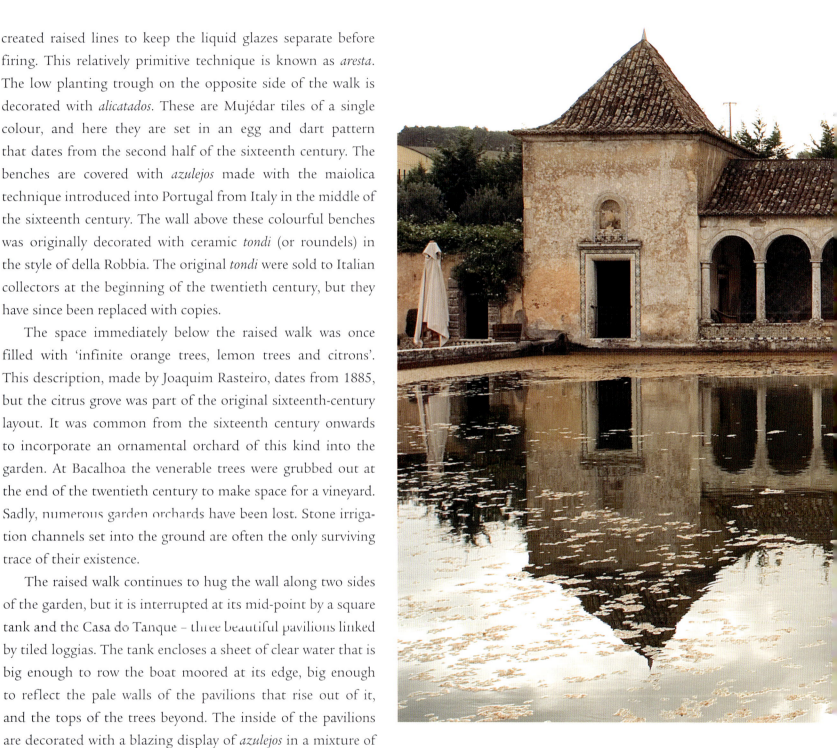

garden. Bacalhoa possesses some of the finest examples of early maiolica tilework in Portugal. The designs were copied from drawings by the Italian artist Enea Vico. In one panel Susanna is shown in the grip of the lascivious elders, and in another Hippodamia struggles to escape rape by Myrtilus. Susanna is

shown in front of a building with the date 1565 inscribed above its door, and this is thought to be the date of production.

The survival of Quinta da Bacalhoa is due largely to Mrs Orlena Scoville, an American who bought the estate in 1936 and undertook a thorough reconstruction of house and garden.

The Casa do Tanque reflected in the still water.

Jardim do Paço Castelo Branco

The bishop's palace and parterre garden seen against a dramatic sky.

Whether you toil down the motorway from Lisbon, or slip over the border from Spain, a visit to the garden of the bishop's palace in Castelo Branco has always been considered obligatory. Alluring photographs capture an extraordinary combination of lichen-covered granite figures, brimming tanks and towering hedges, an image conveying that potent combination of beauty and decay. Something of the old magic has been destroyed in recent years by a thorough cleaning and restoration of all the stonework, a process that has left the pale granite and crude carving of the statues cruelly exposed. Beyond the statues, the stucco facings of the walls have been repainted in a blindingly bright white. Time will eventually repair the damage, toning walls and statues down and reclothing everything with the original soft patina of lichen and moss. Until then a visit to Castelo Branco will continue to be something of a challenge.

The garden of the bishop's palace was built for the Bishop of Guarda, João de Mendonça, in about 1720. The original plans are long gone – they are thought to have been lost during the earthquake of 1755. The name of the garden designer disappeared at the same time. The main garden lies immediately below the palace, which is now a museum. It is an elaborate parterre and a showcase for a large and densely displayed collection of statues. Originally the statues were arranged to convey a series of spiritual messages. Each one stands on an inscribed plinth. Together they represent the seasons (four), the complete cycle of the zodiac (twelve), the continents (four again), and the principal virtues (eight). Box hedges create the structure for this sculpture gallery. They are planted to create neat squares containing the usual complex Portuguese pattern of interlocking shapes. This geometric creation is arranged around a central

ABOVE *The elegant fountains that give the Crown Pool its name.*

RIGHT *The kings of Portugal flank the staircase, their names inscribed on the plinths below.*

fountain and broken up by the random insertion of delight-fully bulky box cubes and drums. Citrus thrives in the enclosed space. Lemons grow as espaliers against the walls, and orange trees with their glowing fruit light up the boundary between the main garden and the adjacent pools.

Two staircases link the main garden to the Moses Terrace immediately above it. The symbolism is quite simple: the Moses Terrace can only be reached by going up the Staircase of the Apostles, or the Staircase of the Doctors of the Church. The granite figures of the apostles flank the steps to each side of

the staircase. They all have wild hair, long beards and bare feet. It is their attributes – the things that they carry or wear – that give the clue to their individual identities. The steps of the staircase on the other side of the garden are flanked by busts of St Jerome, St Gregory, St Ambrose, St Augustine and Pope Leo 'The Great'. Whichever route you take, you will reach the vast and magnificent water tank at the garden's highest level, with its water staircase flanked by elegant granite pillars.

From the far end of the Moses Terrace there is a view over the Crown Pool. This is a generous oblong tank with three fountains formed from elegantly twisted stone columns surmounted by stone crowns. The broad box hedges to each side of the pool are cut into pleasing battlements. There is an irregular space between the Crown Pool and the garden wall known as the Jardim Alagado, or 'flooded garden'. It consists of a pool made in a trapezoid shape that fills the awkward space perfectly. Its eccentric form represents an endearing departure from the traditional regularity of the baroque garden. The garden's name is a reference to the narrow curlicue beds that emerge from the water. In spring these beds blaze with brightly coloured bulbs.

Another magnificent set of stairs leaves the parterre garden at its far end. This is the Kings' Staircase. Again the steps are flanked by stone figures. This time they represent kings of Portugal. The three Spanish kings that ruled the country during the years of Spanish domination do not get a place on the stairs. They are rendered at half size, and they huddle at the base of the steps. The Kings' Staircase led to the Passadiço, the covered bridge that crossed the road, linking the palace garden to the vegetable gardens, olive groves, rabbit enclosures and woods that made up the rest of the property. The bridge – no longer covered – is still there, and today part of this area is laid out as an ornamental park.

LEFT *The stuccoed walls of this tank on the upper terrace were originally frescoed with mythological scenes.*

RIGHT *The raised tank of the Crown Pool at the centre of the garden.*

REAL QUINTA DE CAXIAS

The royal palace and garden of Caxias were built at the beginning of the eighteenth century for Infante Dom Francisco, the younger brother of Dom João V. The garden was part of a much larger project, an estate that grew continuously throughout the eighteenth century until it had gobbled up all the small farms that lay between the garden and the sea. A map of 1844 shows a continuous landscape of neat plantations divided by long avenues that stretched from the garden gates to the Tagus estuary and the Atlantic coast. Francisco was a member of the wealthiest royal family in Europe, a wealth that was fuelled first by the discovery of gold and then of diamonds in Brazil. The garden at Caxias was a royal playground. The family would leave their palace at Queluz, some five miles (eight kilometres) to the north, and travel to Caxias to watch a ballet or play enacted in the garden, listen to a concert, or eat an *alfresco* meal as the heat ebbed away and dusk fell over the garden.

The focal point of the layout is a massive rustic cascade known as the Fountain of Diana. Water descends a series of steep steps clothed in tufa and rough pebble mosaic. Time has been brutal to Machado de Castro's life-size, terracotta statues of Diana and her nymphs. Actaeon's misfortune has been followed by some far greater accident that has left the fountain scattered with nothing but his legs, the armless torso of a fawn and a sprinkling of angry dogs. A terrace suspended above this strange scene supports a pretty tufa-encrusted pavilion, its roof topped by a ceramic stork. Inside the pavilion is a fountain that doubled as a fish tank, with a crystal bowl containing brightly-coloured fish. The pavilion is linked to the lower garden by a web of passages and staircases concealed behind

The Fountain of Diana dominates the garden of the Real Quinta de Caxias.

the cascade. To each side the cascade is flanked by narrow terraces, their retaining walls decorated with painted panels. The top of each retaining wall doubles as a planting trough that is punctuated only by narrow stone seats.

The area between the cascade and the garden walls is entirely filled with magnificent oblong parterres planted in extraordinarily complex patterns made from clipped box. There are fleurs-de-lis enclosed in intricate arabesques and scrolls, linear shapes and fragmented, geometric forms reminiscent of those wooden puzzles that cleverer people can always reassemble. This wonderful landscape can be viewed from the garden terraces, or from the raised pavilions that stand among the beds. From this vantage point oval ponds appear among the parterres, the statues in them representing the four seasons. Smaller, circular bowl fountains are also visible, bright with *azulejos*. The corners of the beds are marked by citrus trees neatly clipped into oval shapes, their trunks concealed by foliage.

The nineteenth century also left its signature on Caxias. This was the century that saw a renewed interest in exotic trees and plants, and two Norfolk Island pines (*Araucaria heterophylla*) tower above this garden as they do over so many other nineteenth-century gardens in the area.

Today the garden belongs to the town council of Oeiras, and since 1993 it has been part of a restoration project promoted by the Commission for European Communities.

LEFT *A deer falls victim to one of Actaeon's hunting dogs on the Fountain of Diana.*

RIGHT *Complex parterres set against a backdrop of neatly clipped orange trees.*

PALÁCIO DOS MARQUESES DA FRONTEIRA

Palácio Fronteira was built during the heady, exuberant period that followed the Wars of Restoration (1641–68). The palace and its magnificent garden were designed for Dom João de Mascarenhas, a key figure in the battle for independence from Spanish rule. Mascarenhas was made first Marquês de Fronteira in recognition of his service as a general during the war. The palace still belongs to the Mascarenhas family.

Dom João and his architect looked to Italy for inspiration. They studied Sebastiano Serlio's *I sette libri dell'architettura*, written in the mid-sixteenth century, where they found the model for the two main facades of the palace. The design of the garden is thought to have been inspired by *Flora, ovvero la cultura dei fiori*, a seventeenth-century Italian florilegium written by Giovanni Battista Ferrari, but the layout lacks the continuity of an Italian garden. It is said that the marquis spent so much on the palace and garden that his son was almost forced to sell the property in order to pay off his father's debts.

In 1755 Lisbon was struck by earthquake, flood and fire, and the Mascarenhas lost their main Lisbon residence at Camões. The city was reduced first to rubble and then, during the slow rebuilding, it became a massive construction site. Most of the aristocracy chose to abandon their ruined palaces and retreat to the suburbs, settling in places like Caxias, Lumiar, Loures, Algés, Carnide and Pedroços. The Marascenhas decided to move into their suburban palace at Benfica. Until then the *palácio* had been a grandiose holiday house, but now it became the family's principal residence and a new wing was built to celebrate the move. No changes were made to the garden.

View across the Great Garden towards the King's Tank.

Palácio Fronteira's garden is like a huge open-air gallery designed to display one of the country's most important collections of seventeenth-century *azulejos*. It is refulgent with tiles that radiate light and colour from the surface of walls, staircases, benches, balustrades and planting troughs. Fronteira was one of the earliest gardens to have *azulejos* specifically designed for it. A few of them are the 'old fashioned' polychrome tiles that were popular until the mid-seventeenth century, but the majority of the tiles in the garden are in the blue and white 'Delft' style. Some of them are genuine Delftware and others are Portuguese imitations. Traditional Dutch tiles were decorated with a single self-contained image, but the Portuguese demanded tiles that could be combined to create the kind of large-scale, pictorial tableaux used all over the garden of Palácio Fronteira. Consequently, the Dutch began to produce tiles specifically for the Portuguese market. In 1670 Dom João de Mascarenhas commissioned a workshop in Amsterdam to produce a series of blue and white tile panels depicting mythological and pastoral scenes for the dining room of the house. These were the first blue and white Dutch tableaux to be imported into Portugal.

ABOVE AND RIGHT *Comic* singerie-*style tiles depicting monkeys running a barber's shop and others teaching music at kitten school.*

Azulejaria dominates the raised terrace that links the palace to the chapel, a short journey, but packed with incident. The long wall running the length of the terrace is entirely clothed in blue and white *azulejos*, and so are the balustrade and the benches on the opposite side of the terrace. *Azulejos* line niches and arches in an extraordinarily complex design that encompasses seven small and six large niches. Inside the larger niches are tableaux depicting the liberal arts – Arithmetic, Rhetoric, Geometry, Music and Astronomy – as serene and buxom women. Poetry is not forgotten, she is enthroned on the east wall of the terrace, a goose at her feet. The presence of these matronly figures gives the terrace its name – The Gallery of the Arts. The smaller, curved niches in the wall are also lined with tiles, but they house life-size marble statues of mythological figures. Add multicoloured, glazed, ceramic roundels of fruit enclosing busts of Roman emperors to this mixture,

EV. SOV.
O MESTRE
DACOLFA

and planting troughs filled with bright flowers, throw in some *azulejos* herms to give support and some *putti* for playfulness, cover the planting toughs with intricate patterns of plants and trees, and set strange birds with human heads to perch in the leafy panels beside the doors. In short, let your imagination run wild over acres of tiles and you will have a sense of this extraordinary *azulejos* extravaganza. The far end of the terrace is enclosed by the façade of the chapel, a fantastic medley of mosaics made from pebbles, coloured glass and broken shards of china. The *casa do fresco* is designed by an equally lavish hand. Legend has it that the china and glass in the mosaics that line its interior were part of a dinner service used at a banquet given in honour of Dom Pedro, the future king, when he visited the palace in 1672. They were broken during a respectful ritual designed to prevent them from ever being used again.

The Garden of Venus lies below the terrace. Terrace and garden are linked by a covered staircase set into the side wall of the chapel. The awkward descent from the terrace alerts the visitor to a profoundly Portuguese aspect of the garden. Each space within the layout is self-contained, and the links between

one space and another are, like the dark staircase, a vacuum, a moment of sensory deprivation in which nothing occurs.

The Garden of Venus is a shade garden, where the shadows of a vast araucaria and ancient magnolias combine with the damp interior of a second *casa do fresco* to give sanctuary from the heat. The walls here and elsewhere in the garden are faced with stucco that is painted a startling Moroccan blue. Nobody knows how long this colour has been used at Palácio de Fronteira, but the inspiration may have come from southern Portugal, where it was traditional to paint the base of house walls blue in the belief that it deterred insects.

The *casa do fresco* is another mosaic extravaganza. Water jets were designed to shoot across the space, landing on the flat stone top of the fountain at its centre. Outside, the backs of the curved stone seats are decorated with a series of comic *azulejos* scenes depicting monkeys engaged in human tasks. *Singerie*, as this style is known, was a very popular form of *azulejos* decoration in the Portuguese garden. The term was coined in France at the beginning of the eighteenth century when Jean Berain, a fashionable designer and decorator, began to include

LEFT *Azulejos* panels of horsemen seen from the King's Pool.

BELOW *Statues of mythological figures surrounded by* azulejos *in the Gallery of the Arts.*

RIGHT *The Great Garden, which was designed to be seen from the first-floor loggia, now enclosed to form the library.*

ABOVE *A twentieth-century azulejos panel designed for the garden by Portuguese artist Paula Rego.*

RIGHT Azulejaria *below the garden wall; the wall is painted blue to deter insects.*

elegantly dressed monkeys in his wall decorations. At Fronteira the scene depicted on the polychrome tiles is of monkeys running a barber's shop. Their customers are small startled cats with round eyes and thin legs. Further along the bench the monkeys are at work in the schoolroom, teaching plump kittens to sing. Above the teacher's head there is a sign reading 'I am the music master'. The base of the bench is decorated with aquatic activities, including coral fishing. The fishermen wear comic goggles. The pool in front of the *casa do fresco* is as unusual as every other aspect of the garden. Shallow and tile lined, the space is broken up by S-shaped islands that are reminiscent of the islands in the ancient Roman pool at Conimbriga (see page 98). Jets of water were designed to play across the stone islands, just as they did in the original Roman garden. The pool is faced with blue and white tiles depicting a watery landscape scene teeming with fish, eels, stingrays, lobsters, turtles and unidentifiable monsters.

The Great Garden occupies the enclosed area to the east of the palace. It was designed to be seen from a first-floor loggia,

a space that was subsequently enclosed and converted into a beautiful airy library. It is only from this perspective that the complexity of the magnificent box parterre can be properly appreciated. A pattern of interlocking beds reminiscent of an elaborate Moorish ceiling is arranged around a central fountain and punctuated by statues and neatly clipped domes and pyramids cut from yew. However, nothing in this decorative display can distract from the Kings' Tank, the climax of the garden and one of the most extraordinary pieces of garden architecture in Portugal. It is a large oblong pool surrounded by an elegant stone balustrade and backed by a retaining wall entirely covered in blue and white *azulejos*. Spring water wells up, quietly and continuously, through a black hole in the base of the tank. Staircases at each end of the pool lead up through square pavilions to an upper terrace. The retaining wall behind the pool is divided into twelve panels that depict life-size figures riding spirited horses. The horses' bodies are slightly foreshortened, creating the dramatic impact of Velasquez's equestrian portraits. The riders wear elegant feathered hats and their sashes billow behind them. The upper terrace is called the Galeria dos Reis (Gallery of the Kings). Busts of Portugal's kings are arranged in apses lined with fascinating relief *azulejos* made in blue and white or an iridescent bronze lustre. These dazzlingly beautiful tiles, with their strange pine-cone motif, are unique to this wonderful place. From the terrace it is possible to steal a glimpse of the area behind the garden that was once filled with vegetable plots and ornamental orchards. Although nothing is left of the original layout, lemon, almond and fig trees still grow there, evoking the images from a seventeenth-century poem by Richard Flecknoe that describes the beauty of Portugal's pleasure orchards:

With the most beautiful gardens full
Of delightful fruit-bearing trees
Such as the orange, the lemon, the damson and the peach,
Mulberries with wide-spreading branches which give us silk,
Fig trees and hundreds of others.

QUINTA DE MONSERRATE

In 1790 Gerard de Visme signed a nine-year lease on Monserrate. This was the beginning of a process that transformed a small rural estate outside Sintra into an extravagant, Anglo-Portuguese, romantic garden with a bizarre nineteenth-century palace at its heart. De Visme was an old friend of the Marquis of Pombal, and consequently he had been granted the monopoly for importing Brazilian teak. This lucrative concession made him the richest man in the English Factory. By the time he took on Monserrate he had already built a fine neo-classical mansion at Benfica, outside Lisbon. When William Hickey, traveller and connoisseur, stayed with him in 1782 he found him living in a 'princely' establishment. William Beckford said that the garden at Benfica 'eclipses all the lead statues, Chinese temples, winding rivers and old chapels of Bagnigge Wells, White Conduit House and Marleybone...'

The lease of Monserrate obliged de Visme to restore the orchards, repair existing structures and build a new house. In 1791 the new house was built on the site. De Visme is thought to have commissioned the English architect William Elsden to design the new palace, which was the first gothic revival building in Portugal. It was a long building with a square castellated tower at its centre and circular turrets at either end. When William Beckford saw it in 1794 he described it as 'barbarous gothic built by a carpenter from Falmouth'. The reference to carpentry was a characteristic piece of Beckford nastiness, a remark based on a flimsy rumour that Elsden had been a cabinet maker before boarding ship in Falmouth and embarking upon his illustrious career as the Marquis of Pombal's architect of choice.

De Visme's tenure was short-lived. In 1795 ill health obliged him to exchange Sintra for Wimbledon. There had hardly been

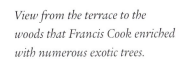

View from the terrace to the woods that Francis Cook enriched with numerous exotic trees.

time to make an impact on the garden landscape. However, he was known by his contemporaries for his 'particular genius for agriculture', and it seems possible that he installed the efficient irrigation system that survives in part to this day. Spring water collected on the hills is transported in terracotta channels running along the tops of the low walls that thread through the garden. These channels can be blocked with a sandbag, causing the water to overflow onto the ground wherever it is needed. It is essentially an Arabic system of the kind used in Portugal since the eighth century.

Despite his criticism of the new house, Beckford had no hesitation in taking on the lease from de Visme. His journal of 1787-88 reveals that he was already smitten by the Portuguese landscape:

> The scenery is truly Elysian, and worthy to be the lounge of happy souls ... the vivid green of the citron, the golden fruitage of the orange, the blossoming myrtle and the rich fragrance of the turf, embroidered with aromatic flowers allow me without a violent stretch of fancy to believe myself in the garden of the Hesperides, and to expect a dragon under every tree.

Of Monserrate he said, 'It was a beautiful, Claude-like place, surrounded by the most enchanting country.' He remained a sub-tenant for several years, visiting the house many times and living there throughout 1794. The dramatic landscape with its deep-sided valley lent itself to romantic treatment. In 1795 Beckford described himself as:

> too much engaged with the Royalty of Nature, with climbing roses and cork trees, with tracing rills and runnels to their source, and examining every recess of these lovely environs, to think of lesser royalties.

LEFT *Ferns, lichens and other damp-lovers colonize the trunks and branches of mature trees.*

RIGHT *The neo-gothic windows, Moorish carving and exotic roofline of Monserrate.*

This 'tracing' of 'rills and runnels' inspired the cascade that was his most imposing contribution to the landscape. The water tears down a dramatic, boulder-strewn ravine, twisting and turning on its way to the shady valley below. Beckford intensified the natural drama of the landscape by adding picturesque details to it. His cromlech (megalithic tomb) still stands beside the path from the road to the house, and he built a neo-gothic ruined chapel among the trees, using the stone of a real chapel destroyed during the earthquake of 1755.

Beckford eventually tired of Portugal, and by the time Byron visited Monserrate in 1809 he was gone. The deserted house was already descending into dereliction, its abandoned garden overgrown. By 1821 Mariana Baillie was able to describe the place as, 'completely a ruin; a fit residence only for bat and owl...' However, Monserrate's glory days were still to come, when the estate was bought in 1856 by Sir Francis Cook. Cook was an English textile merchant who had amassed an enormous fortune in Portugal. He commissioned James Knowles, a fashionable English architect, to renovate the building, and it is his extraordinarily elaborate and heavily ornamented design

that we see at Monserrate today. Knowles decided to leave the house that Visme had built in place, but he overlayed the structure with details that Rose Macaulay described as 'barbarous orientalism ... constructed in a Moorish delirium'. It was an expression of all that was romantic and exotic in the English imagination. Indoors, de Visme's neo-gothic decorations were restored and mixed with plasterwork inspired by the Alhambra, balustrades looted during the Indian Mutiny, exotically carved pillars, mosaics and friezes. Cook lived at Monserrate like a Victorian country gentleman, devoting time and money to the garden that he traversed on a donkey and to an array of local charities. An enormous workforce was needed to rebuild the house and to build and maintain the garden. Cook provided medical care for his employees and built two primary schools for their children. This enlightened behaviour attracted the attention of the king, who awarded him the title of Visconde de Monserrate.

Cook was a collector and the house was soon filled with superb paintings, antiques and oriental furniture. The impulse to collect followed him from house to garden,

LEFT *Neo-moorish tiles decorate the fountains in the garden.*

RIGHT *Francis Cook built up layers of contrasting forms and foliage to create a dense, subtropical forest.*

LEFT *Ornate stone steps link the house to the lower garden, the woods and the ruined chapel.*

RIGHT *Rhododendrons flower beneath the dense canopy created by the oaks.*

where the woods and the park became the setting for a vast collection of shrubs and trees from all over the world, many of them donated by the botanic gardens of Kew, Lisbon and Rio de Janeiro. Cook was particularly fond of evergreens, and Monserrate is full of palms, pines, cypresses and conifers of every description. He worked alongside Francis Burt, the gardener from his father's estate in Kent, and together they divided the site up into areas representing New Zealand, Australia, China, Japan, Mexico, Peru and Africa, filling each one with plants that thrived in Sintra's magical climate. An account published in *The Times* in 1886 creates a vivid impression of Cook's achievement:

> Here huge American aloes throw up their tall flower laden masts high in the air, grouped with strange cactus and prickly pears, tall palms, araucarias and New Zealand tree ferns. There entire groves and thickets of camellias, laden with myriads of splendid flowers; tropical climbing plants like the splendid bougainvillea from Brazil, hang from tree to tree in vast sheets, rivers and pendant festoons of purple flowers; whilst roses and scarlet passion flowers run for 100 feet or so ahead among the trees, matted together in glorious and bewildering confusion.

During the 1920s the estate belonged to Sir Herbert Cook, Francis Cook's grandson, who replanted part of the garden. He poached Walter Oates, head gardener at La Mortola in Italy, persuading him to come to Monserrate and direct the restoration. This was another fine period for the garden, but by 1929 the estate was up for sale for £200,000. It was not until 1947, however, that the family found a buyer for the entire estate, including the contents of the house. The buyer proved to be a speculator who stripped the assets before selling the empty house to the Portuguese state in 1949. It has remained empty and the garden, maintained under Sir Herbert Cook by 72 full-time gardeners, struggles for survival. However, Monserrate has many fans, and the Friends of Monserrate is an energetic organisation formed to promote public awareness and raise funds for maintenance and restoration of house and garden.

A glimpse of the gate piers that flank the entrance to an area originally used for growing vegetables.

PALÁCIO DO MARQUÊS DE POMBAL

Palácio do Marquês de Pombal was the summer palace of Sebastião José de Carvalho e Melo, Count of Oeiras and Marquis of Pombal. This is to say, it was the home of the most powerful figure in eighteenth-century Portugal, a man whose political career spanned nearly forty years, over twenty of them as prime minister and effective ruler of the country. This is no place to list Pombal's achievements, to consider the slow revolution that he worked upon the country's backward economy and its blinkered education system, or to describe the draconian measures that he took against the Jesuits and the aristocracy. However, Pombal's ruthlessly enforced reforms did play a significant role in the history of Portuguese gardens. In the mid-eighteenth century the country's aristocracy consisted of only nine marquises, thirty-three counts and a handful of dukes. This was Portugal's chief garden-owning and garden-making class. In his determination to dismantle the traditional system of privileges Pombal virtually annihilated the old aristocracy and, stripped of guaranteed positions at court, of embassies, governorships and other lucrative offices, they could no longer afford to create gardens, or to maintain the gardens that they had owned for generations in Lisbon or on their country estates.

Pombal took possession of the Carvalho family's fertile estate in Oeiras on the death of his first wife in 1737. He commissioned Carlos Mardel to design both the palace and the garden. Mardel was a Hungarian who had made his name by collaborating on the design of the Aguas Livres aqueduct in Lisbon, and was then appointed as one of the principal

architects during the reconstruction of the city after the earthquake of 1755. The marquis commissioned a palace and a second house further up the hill. This is the Quinta de Cima, where the fertile ground surrounding the house was planted with orchards, and barns were built to house silkworms. In the garden there is a large tank with a pavilion beside it. The *Casa da Pesca*, or fishing pavilion, was faced with blue-and-white *azulejos* panels based on drawings by Claude Joseph Vernet. The principal tableau depicts the antics of nymphs and sea gods in a watery landscape.

Further down the hill the garden of the summer palace was designed as a setting for games, plays, ballets and concerts – all the light-hearted pastimes of the summer months. A boating canal and a bowling alley were built within easy reach of the palace. The house stands on a raised terrace overlooking the main garden. The terrace is a quintessentially Portuguese garden space, crammed with complex box parterres, elegantly sculpted hunting dogs, classical statues and shallow pools. The pink walls of the house enclose it on two sides, and on the third the low retaining wall is faced with glowing *azulejos*. Palácio de

View down the main axis of the garden to the Poet's Cascade.

the terrace is decorated with yellow, marbled *azulejos* of the kind produced by Rato, the royal tile factory in Lisbon. They are decorated with cherubs, rococo patterns and a hunting scene involving young men in fashionable hats. The terrace is linked to the main garden by three highly ornate staircases. The principal staircase corresponds with the main axis of the garden. It is decorated with polychrome tiles and wrought-iron balustrades. A second staircase leads to the Araucaria Terrace, where pale statues stand out against the dark trunks of towering Norfolk Island pines. On this staircase the tiles are blue and white, but they are surrounded by a polychrome border of fluted forms, leaves and shells.

The garden's main axis runs from the principal staircase to the Poet's Cascade. It passes the shady bowling alley where Queen Maria I is said to have played in 1783. What was the queen doing playing bowls in the garden of her old enemy? The marquis was dead by then, but she had disliked him enough to issue an injunction that forbade him to come within twenty miles of her, and shortly afterwards she banished him from Oeiras to the isolated village of Pombal. Beyond the bowling alley the path crosses the boating canal that snakes around the garden perimeter. An *azulejos* panel conveys a vivid impression of the fine boating parties that would have taken place on it. A vast open space stretches between the bridge and the Poet's Cascade. Empty space was not a feature of Portuguese garden design in the eighteenth century, and this one was originally filled by orange, lemon and almond trees. Ornamental orchards of this kind had been a fundamental element of the Portuguese garden since the sixteenth century, but here the orchard provoked scathing remarks from foreign visitors. Shame on William Dalrymple for saying that the 'great rows of orange and lemon trees' had been 'set out in a tasteless manner', and on Arthur Costigan for thinking that they reflected a mundane desire on the designer's part to 'make use of everything'. How much offence they could have avoided if they had bothered to understand the powerful effect of citrus on the Portuguese imagination, its romantic association with

Pombal was built at a watershed in the history of tile making. French rococo colours and styles began to leech into the *azulejaria* tradition from about 1730, and gradually blue-and-white tiles gave way to polychrome designs in yellow, green and the deep, aubergine purple that can be obtained from manganese oxide. The images on these tiles were graceful, insubstantial and delicately drawn. This was the era of Watteau and the *fête galante*, of boating parties, al fresco dances, picnics and hunting scenes These activities became the common theme of rococo *azulejaria* in the garden. At Palácio de Pombal the low wall of

LEFT *A back view of the river
god from inside the Poet's Cascade.
The palace is visible beyond the trees.*

BELOW *A hollow wall doubles
as a planting trough – a traditional
feature in the Portuguese garden.*

RIGHT *Blue and white*
azulejos *decorate the steps that
link the Araucaria Terrace to the
lower garden.*

ancient Arabic gardens, with poetry and Portugal's golden
age of discovery. And how much better they would have liked
Pombal's garden if they had lingered long enough to appreciate
the scent of citrus blossom and to enjoy the glancing light
reflected by the trees' glossy leaves.

The Poet's Cascade lies at the far end of the garden's
main axis. It is the rustic underwater palace of a river god built
from huge lumps of volcanic rock and encrusted with mosaics.
The whole structure was built to be doused in water that tumbled from its summit and crashed into the pool below, bathing
the lithe body of the river god who lounges at its base. He is
said to be modelled on a sculpture from Rome's Cortile del
Belvedere. Rome may be in his bloodline, but he looks distinctly
Portuguese in this extraordinary setting. The ground and the
shady grottos behind the cascade are covered in pebble mosaics,
and the pavilions to either side of it are crowned by the busts of
Homer, Tasso, Virgil and the great Portuguese author Camões.
These were executed by Machado de Castro, whom Pombal also
commissioned to make the equestrian statue of Dom José I that
stands in Lisbon's Praça do Comércio.

Robillion's dolphin fountain in the Garden of Malta, outside the throne room.

PALÁCIO DE QUELUZ

The Queluz estate lies on the banks of the Rio do Jamor, between Lisbon and Sintra. Originally there was nothing on the site but a simple hunting lodge surrounded by vineyards and orchards. All that changed in 1746 when the Infante Dom Pedro embarked on the first stage of a project that would last sixty years and transform Queluz into a magnificent summer palace surrounded by gardens. The palace became Dom Pedro's sanctuary from the monotony and ostentation of life in the royal court of Lisbon. It was built for privacy, relaxation, and entertainment, a place for children to run free and courtships to flourish. Mateus Vicente's design for the palace is a perfect expression of purpose. It leaves the public empty handed, turning its back on the road and saving the beauty of its main façade for the garden. During the long, hot summer days and nights, this garden became a vast outdoor playroom, equipped with every imaginable form of entertainment. Visiting it today is a little like going to a theatre, but the stage seems strangely empty. Although the set is largely intact, many of the beautiful props – the painted and gilded lead statues, the elaborate wooden pavilions, the miniature carriages used by the princes and princesses, the aviaries and the elegant gondolas with their tasselled canopies – are gone.

The rose-coloured walls of the main façade create the backdrop for Jean-Baptiste Robillion's Garden of Neptune. This is the main garden at Queluz, and the most formal element of the entire layout. Robillion was a brilliant Frenchman, an architect, sculptor, decorator and goldsmith. He engaged with both the palace and the garden, creating such a powerful visual and structural link between them that the garden became a natural extension of the indoor rooms. A handsome stone balustrade

surrounds the garden, and this enclosure enhances the sense that it is simply another palatial room. Robillion built on the link between garden and palace by adding decorative details with a horticultural theme to the façade. Lavish rococo garlands and cornucopias overflowing with flowers were carved from limestone to his design, and added to the window surrounds and the pediment. The garden's main axis is centred on this façade. Today it is flanked by low geometric parterre beds of clipped box, but Robillion's original layout was made up of *broderie* arabesques, a style that would have married perfectly with the rococo design of the Fountain of Neptune at the centre of the garden, and with his decorations on the palace. The Fountain of Neptune and the smaller pools set among the parterres were fed with a copious supply of water brought to Queluz from the surrounding hills in ingenious stone-lined channels and aqueducts.

The green parterre garden with its stone balustrade soon became an extraordinary open-air sculpture gallery. The scale on which Dom Pedro commissioned and bought garden statues was quite astounding. After his first order was placed in London in 1755 seventy-six cases of lead statues were

ABOVE Azulejos *decorate every surface of the boating canal, inside and out.*

RIGHT *A marble sphinx which was probably imported from Italy.*

dispatched. The following year a further fifty-eight cases were sent off, shortly before a third order of eighty-nine figures was placed. The majority of these lead statues were made by John Cheere in his yard on Hyde Park Corner in London. John Cheere's Neptune, with his retinue of sea nymphs, dolphins, fish and serpents, creates the central focus of the garden, but all the smaller pools and parterres were also richly decorated with lead figures of shepherds and shepherdesses, pastoral deities, animals, and characters from the *commedia dell'arte* tradition. As if this was not enough, a large collection of marble statues was imported from Italy to adorn the garden balustrade. Beyond the balustrade garden gives way to park. Here the grand 'Frenchness' of Robillion's layout develops into something more introverted, more private and intrinsically Portuguese. Queluz is often compared to Versailles, but at Versailles a broad ride setting off meaningfully towards the road would be met by a monumental gateway. Here the central axis that cuts through

the garden and the park loses conviction at the last minute. Instead of meeting the road it ducks down behind an immense cascade that entirely conceals it from the outside world. This cascade was designed to be a culmination of the main axis, and it was the climax of Robillion's design. The water fell from two stone masks, and tore over huge boulders before tumbling dramatically into the basin far below. The park spread out to either side of the cascade, and many of the trees in it were imported from Holland. Dutch trees were shipped in vast cargoes. From 1755-56 alone, 800 lime trees were imported from Holland, along with chestnuts and elms. Seeds, garden tools, and even a Dutch head gardener were included in the consignment.

The second phase of building began in 1758, just before Dom Pedro's marriage to his niece, Dona Maria I. This phase saw the creation of Robillion's Garden of Malta outside the throne room. The garden is said to have been named in honour of the Knights of Malta when they invited Dom Pedro to join the brotherhood. A sunken area immediately outside the throne room was originally occupied by a large water tank. Robillion replaced this with an oval pool, giving it a decorative, undulating edge. The lead fountain at the centre of the pool depicts two frivolous cherubs struggling to hold onto a leaping a dolphin. Five steps link the pool to the main garden. Robillion designed a delicately curved profile for them that echoes the design of the pool. The main body of the Garden of Malta is filled with parterres made from clipped box, laurel and myrtle, and by topiary pyramids and figures, all imported from Holland. There was once a large collection of animal sculptures in this part of the garden, a menagerie that included monkeys, foxes, hounds, lions and cockerels.

Dona Maria I, whose madness eventually soured the atmosphere at Queluz, and her husband Dom Pedro were both fascinated by botany, and in particular by the exotic plants sent to Queluz from Brazil. In 1769 a botanic garden was established near the cascade, with greenhouses for exotic plants. A wooden arch in the shape of a pagoda formed the entrance to this area, There is nothing to be seen of it today, but an inventory of 1798 lists numerous rare and exotic trees, plants and shrubs grown here and elsewhere in the park. The list includes magnolias, a rare variety of geranium from South Africa and an Asian cinnamon tree. Dom Pedro continued to import crates of bulbs, plants and seeds from Holland. Among them were hundreds of ranunculus corms – 900 were imported in February 1781 alone.

Robillon had added a new wing to the palace. A powerfully theatrical staircase linked this end of the building to an area of the garden set aside for entertainment. You might have sought this route on a hot summer night if, driven out by the heat trapped inside the palace, you craved the cool air that hung over the canal. The canal was best seen at night, when the water turned to liquid gold in the light of a thousand flickering candles. The orchestra warmed up at dusk, and by nightfall ethereal music drifted through the open doors of the wooden pavilion on the bridge. Gondolas floated up and down, carrying a precious cargo of princes and princesses. Lucky them – as they lay back among cushions they could gaze out at a blue and white arcadian landscape unfolding before their eyes. The *azulejos* panels were designed by João Nunes, and they covered the entire length of the canal. The tiles continue on the external walls and benches, but here they are polychrome and depict boating parties at Queluz and numerous other *fêtes galantes*.

If magic still clings to the canal today, when the sluice gates are broken, and the *azulejos* panels hang in mid air high above a muddy stream, imagine the enchanted atmosphere of the garden at its zenith. The royal family lived a secluded, informal life at Queluz, but they were surrounded by magnificence, and the long summer days must have passed quickly in a succession of glorious entertainments. Generations of royal children flourished here, and Dona Carlota herself was only ten years old when she was drafted in from Spain to marry eighteen-year-old Dom João. (Incidentally, she took an immediate dislike to him, and is said to have returned his tentative kiss on the cheek with a vicious bite on the ear). The princes and princesses raced around the park in miniature carriages, visiting their own little patches of garden, peeping at the lions and tigers in the menagerie and stopping to feed the pretty Brazilian birds that each of them kept in their very own aviaries. Should Dona Carlota spend a

Geraldo José Van den Kolk, the king's Dutch gardener, is thought to have introduced the first topiary to the Garden of Malta.

morning in the billiard room, or was this a better day for a game of quoits in the shady bowling alley with its tile-lined seats? Should Dom João go to the octagonal riding school to practise his tilting, or should he sit in the royal box of the miniature bull-ring and enjoy an exhilarating bullfight? Every royal birthday and the birth of each prince and princess were celebrated with an opera performed in a wooden pavilion in the garden court-yard. The gardens were often illuminated with tin lanterns for parties, and feast days were celebrated with fireworks, horse races and bullfights. The painting of a party held during the 1770s shows an outdoor stage draped with a gold awning and crowded with acrobats, musicians and masked figures.

In 1794 a fire in the royal palace of Ajuda resulted in Queluz becoming the official royal residence. By this time Maria I was in the grip of a terrible melancholy, and her screams echoed through the corridors of the palace, terrifying visitors. As ever, William Beckford captured the atmosphere in a vivid and perhaps partially accurate vignette:

> The beings who wandered about this limbo belonged chiefly to that species of living furniture which encumber royal palaces – walking chairs, animated screens, commodes and conveniences, to be used by sovereigns in any manner they like best... weather-beaten equerries, superannuated *véadors* [chamberlains], and wizened pages.

By the end of November 1807 Napoleonic troops had invaded the country and Dom João, his family and their entire retinue had fled Portugal for Brazil. Their chaotic departure was described by one of the courtiers:

> If you looked to one side you could see a mass of belongings lying exposed to the elements; on the other, ornate carriages, waiting for the [royal] family, rode about aimlessly abandoning the protocol usually accorded these occasions, some not wanting to be separated from their luggage and servants ... others eager to get going ... frightened they were running out of time ... It was like this we left Queluz ...

This was an exodus, and the family took an extraordinary quantity of luggage. The royal treasury went with them, along with hundreds of government files containing records that stretched back for centuries. Among the papers was half the archive relating to the palace and gardens of Queluz. It remains in Brazil to this day. When the family finally sailed out of Lisbon, the dock was covered in crates of books, sodden papers and carriages still laden with valuables for the French to find. The palace was abandoned, and behind its rain-streaked walls the rooms lay empty. Perhaps it is better to remember the gardens in better times, described, once again, by William Beckford:

> The evening was now drawing towards its final close, and the groves, pavilions and aviaries now sinking apace into shadow... Cascades and fountains were in full play; a thousand sportive *jets d'eau* were sprinkling the rich masses of bay and citron, and drawing forth all their odours...

Manini exploited the contrast between rustic granite and ação – the finest white limestone – in the garden.

QUINTA DA REGALEIRA

This is what happens when a set designer exchanges the paint and plywood, controlled lighting and stale air of the theatre for the realities of cloud and shifting sunlight, stone, water, grass, trees and flowers. This is what happened when Luigi Manini, an Italian who had become the greatest set designer in Portugal, was commissioned to make his fantasies a reality.

Manini began his career at La Scala in Milan before moving to Lisbon and the São Carlos Theatre in 1879. Opera was already his speciality, but when the curtain lifted on his first set the audience greeted it with a long silence followed by a storm of stamping and catcalls. They were accustomed to old fashioned and repetitive designs, and at first they were repelled by Manini's novel approach and his vibrant palette. Within the year, however, he had become their hero. The naturalistic style that had initially evoked nothing but disgust soon became so popular that there was scarcely a theatre in the land without a set designed by Manini. The Portuguese took to Manini in the nineteenth century just as they had taken to the Italian architect Niccolò Nasoni a hundred years before (see page 21). Nasoni introduced Portugal to the baroque garden, and Manini brought romantic landscape design to its climax at Regaleira.

In 1898 Manini was commissioned by Dr António Augusto Carvalho Monteiro to rebuild the palace of Regaleira on the outskirts of Sintra, and to remodel and greatly extend the existing garden. Carvalho Monteiro was the ideal patron. As an opera lover he applauded Manini's scenographic approach to design, and money was no object. He had inherited an enormous fortune and expanded it through trade in Brazilian coffee and precious stones. He was an enthusiastic collector of antiques, shells, clocks and butterflies, and he owned one of the finest

LEFT AND ABOVE *Manini's garden mosaics sometimes incorporated the initials of his patron, Carvalho Monteiro.*

RIGHT *The circular staircase encircling the well descends for nearly 100 feet (30 metres).*

libraries in Portugal. Manini worked for him for twelve years, and might well have continued but for the assassination of King Carlos and the transformation of Portuguese society after the creation of the Republic.

When Monteiro bought Regaleira in 1893 there was already a villa on the site, surrounded by orchards, coppices and extensive glasshouses. Manini's commission was a licence to rebuild the house and to utterly transform the gardens. This was not his first experience of architecture. In 1888 he had been commissioned by Queen Maria Pia to provide drawings for the

enormous palace at Bussaco (see page 54). Both Bussaco and Regaleira demanded the highest standards of stonemasonry. The team of stonecutters, sculptors and stonemasons working with Manini at Bussaco had served their apprenticeship at the Escola Livre das Artes e Desenho in Coimbra, where they became expert in working with limestone. Manini called up the same highly skilled team to work with him at Regaleira. They were first engaged in 1900 during the remodelling of the stable block. This was followed by the construction of a chapel covered in an embroidery of extraordinarily ornate carving and decorated with statues. The palace was their greatest challenge. Its elaborate neo-gothic façade is decorated with finely carved pinnacles, buttresses and towers, every door and window is surrounded by a filigree of carving and the roof line is decorated with an enormous range of gargoyles. Much of this stonework was created in the workshop of João Machado in Coimbra, before being transported to Sintra by train. Manini designed the entrance to the garden with great care. The house remains hidden until you have progressed some way up the drive. Then it is suddenly revealed in all its bizarre glory, the first of many surprises.

It is not easy to put words around the vast but intricate landscape that unfolds on the hillside above the palace, to convey the massive scale and minute detail of Manini's vision, or the mysterious atmospheres that infuse the extravagant follies and the winding paths. Manini remained a set designer at heart. He always worked to create maximum impact and to produce a great concentration of effects. His audiences never had time to tire of one set before it was replaced by another, and this was the technique that he employed in the garden. He was capable of inventing fantastic scenes and of turning them into reality. The sheer range of structures in the garden is startling. Among the follies, the granite tower at the centre of the landscape is the most important structure. However, the woods surrounding it are full of other surprises. The towering trees frame delicately carved, limestone exedras and belvederes, staircases, neo-manueline gateways, fountains, naturalistic pools and cascades. Even the storerooms, greenhouses, incinerator and the other service buildings were dressed up to create a picturesque effect. The buildings became the focal point of a series of carefully composed sets that still lie concealed among the trees. In the theatre Manini was a 'total designer', that is to say that he took responsibility for every aspect of the scenery. Outside in the garden he exercised a similar degree of control. He achieved this through the use of perspective, creating a series of minutely controlled views. Buildings, staircases or cascades were concealed by trees or by landscape itself until a moment of Manini's choosing. When that moment came, he revealed his creations as a series of delightful and unexpected surprises.

Many of Manini's carefully controlled effects have survived to this day, but some of the views have, perhaps inevitably, become obscured by overgrown trees. Plants thrive in the warmth and humidity of Sintra's magical microclimate, many of them taking on a romantic patina of ferns, lichen or moss. Manini's planting palette was as exotic as his architecture. He planted trees and shrubs from all over the world, blending them into the natural vegetation of the hillside and creating picturesque combinations of water, rock and greenery. Water is crucial to Regaleira. Like most other *quintas* in Sintra,

LEFT *Statues punctuate the formal hedges of the lower garden.*

RIGHT *Tree ferns reach an enormous size in Sintra's magical microclimate.*

Regaleira had the water rights over areas of higher ground. However, when Monteiro Carvalho acquired the property he realised that the existing water supply would be insufficient for the new palace and its vast and ambitious gardens. He was quick to purchase disused rights belonging to neighbouring properties and he commissioned the construction of a system of aqueducts to carry the water to the estate. Consequently, the garden is rich in still pools of clear springwater, rushing streams, cascades and dripping grottos. The garden is a paradise for the ducks and swans that live in it. Some of their most impressive accommodation is provided by a large pond at the garden's lowest level. Water fills the pond and an *enfilade* of caves carved out of the cliff face. The caves are clad in a mixture of a naturally pitted stone brought by the trainload from Peniche, and a false limestone cleverly created by dripping sulphuric acid onto builders' rubble. The dramatic structure of the caves and the flickering shadows on the rock walls create a wonderfully theatrical atmosphere.

For sheer drama, however, nothing can rival the circular well that extends below ground level for ninety-nine dark and dripping feet (thirty metres). The entrance is a 'secret' stone door, a wonderfully theatrical piece of engineering that swings open onto a dark, grotto-like interior. A spiral staircase encircles the well and leads to its base and the web of cavernous, granite tunnels that were blasted out of the hillside to link it to the outside world. Originally these tunnels were lit and partially lit by tiny coloured lanterns. Today the lighting is still subtle, and sometimes non-existent, the tunnels are dark and damp, and it is a relief to emerge into the sunshine. Water flows over the entrance to the tunnel and falls into a beautifully made, naturalistic pool that it appears to have been worn from the living rock. In some respects Manini seems to have worked like the architects of the Italian Renaissance. He was intent first on imitating and then on outdoing nature, creating 'natural' forms that are actually exaggerated, like the features of a theatre set.

Manini left Portugal for Italy in 1912. The *quinta* has passed through the hands of numerous owners, the garden has suffered neglect and endured restoration, but its quirky soul survives, vibrant and intact.

The building of Palácio de Seteais was completed while William Beckford was living near Sintra in the Quinta do Ramalhão. He had already formed a strong alliance with Mrs Gildermeester. 'She is not of the merciful kind', he said, 'and she spares nobody'. Her mockery of the English merchants' wives was exactly to his taste, and they stuck together at dances and dinners. When Beckford was invited to the Gildermeester's house-warming party he travelled through 'dark lanes' to the house, where he found:

little more than bare walls, and wretchedly lighted up....' In several of the apartments – you will hardly believe me – one woeful candle depended from the ceiling in a solitary lantern. I leave you to represent to yourself the effect of this stable-like decoration.

Not what he had expected from one of the richest hosts in the country, and a hostess who, unsurprisingly, dripped with diamonds. Fortunately, he was much cheered by the dining room:

...there was bright illumination, a profusion of plate, a striking breadth of table, every delicacy that could be procured, and a dessert frame 50 to 60 feet in length, gleaming with burnished figures and vases of silver flowers of the most exquisite workmanship.

Daniel Gildermeester died in 1793, and in 1800 his son sold Palácio de Seteais to Dom Diogo José Vito de Meneses Noronha Coutinho, the fifth Count of Marialva. The count built the second pavilion and the triumphal arch that links the two buildings. The arch was built in honour of a visit by the future king Dom João VI and Dona Carlota. The cobbled road between the buildings leads to a stone seat in the wall and a view over a second parterre garden and the sea beyond it. Today the palace is a hotel, and the gardens are beautifully maintained.

ABOVE The main entrance was originally on this side of the palace, overlooking the ornamental citrus orchard.

RIGHT Parterres below the second pavilion, built by the fifth Count of Marialva.

PALÁCIO DE SETEAIS

Palácio de Seteais is set back from the lane that leads from Sintra to Colares. It was built in 1783 by Daniel Gildermeester, the Dutch consul. Rather like de Visme at Monserrate, Gildermeester had a close relationship with the Marquis of Pombal and as a consequence he was given the monopoly on the export of Brazilian diamonds. Gildermeester bought the land at Seteais from Pombal and secured permission to quarry the granite needed for the building. Today the house is made up of two pavilions linked by a triumphal arch. Gildermeester's palace was the left-hand pavilion. It is an elegant, neo-classical building set into the side of the hill. The wide level lawn that separates it from the road was originally used as a parade ground for soldiers. The original entrance to the palace building was at the side, where a long stone terrace looks inland over an ornamental citrus orchard. Beyond the orchard the hill rises steeply. The Pena Palace creates a wonderful climax to the view.

Today the hillside is clad in a dense covering of trees, but originally it was cut into a series of open terraces that were linked by steps and furnished with grottos and pavilions. Winter gales batter the parterre garden on the seaward side of the building, stunting the trees and leeching colour from the paintwork on the palace doors and windows. It is a hanging garden, suspended above the plain, and nothing obstructs the view between it and the sea. The neatly clipped parterres are planted in box and arranged around a simple bowl fountain. To one side of the parterre there is a small square enclosure surrounded by a low wall. Stone seats are set into the wall, suggesting that the area was set aside for chatting, and enjoying the magnificent view.

The parterre garden on the seaward side of Palácio de Seteais.

BIBLIOGRAPHY

Marianne Baillie, *Lisbon in the Years 1821, 1822 and 1823*, London, 1824

William Edward Baxter, *The Tagus and the Tiber, 1850–1851*

William Dalrymple, *Travels through Spain and Portugal in 1774*, London, 1777

Robert M. Gimson, 'Further ventilation on the history of the Oporto camellias', *International Camellia Journal*, 11, 1979

Malcolm Jack, *Sintra: A Glorious Eden*, Carcanet, 2002

J. A. Levenson, *The Age of the Baroque in Portugal*

H. F. Link, *Voyage en Portugal, depuis 1797 jusqu'en 1799*, Paris, 1803-5

Frederick G. Meyer, 'Plant explorations – ornamentals in Italy, Southern France, Spain, Portugal, England and Scotland', *Crop Research*, 34-9, U.S. Department of Agriculture, October 1959

James C. Murphy, *Travels in Portugal; Through the Provinces of Entre Douro e Minho, Beira, Estremadura, and Alem-Tejo, In the Years 1789 and 1790. Consisting of Observations on the Manner, Customs, Trade, Public Buildings, Arts, Antiquities, &c. of that Kingdom*, London, 1795

Charles Quest Ritson, *The English Garden Abroad*, Viking, 1992

Joaquim Rasteiro, *Quinta e Palácio da Bacalhoa em Azeitão*, Lisbon, 1885

Charles Sellers, *Oporto Old and New*, Herbert E Harper, 1899.

L.F. de Tollenare, *Notes dominicales prises pendant un voyage en Portugal et au Brésil en 1816, 1817 et 1818*, Calouste Gulbenkian Foundation, Paris, 1971-73

Patrick Wilken, *Empire Adrift. The Portuguese Court in Rio de Janeiro 1808–1821*, Bloomsbury, 2004

LEFT *Subtropical planting at Monserrate, where agaves are backed by 'bird of paradise' flowers (*Strelitzia reginae*).*

INDEX

Numbers in **bold** refer to illustrations.

*The blue and white tiles on the seats at
Quinta dos Azulejos are surrounded
by fanciful rococo frames.*